SIR PHILIP SIDNEY

SIR PHILIP SIDNEY

Selected Writings
Astrophil and Stella, The Defence of Poesy and Miscellaneous Poems

*Edited with an introduction and Notes
by Richard Dutton*

Fyfield*Books*

For Katie

First published in Great Britain 1987 by
Carcanet Press Limited
208-212 Corn Exchange Buildings
Manchester M4 3BQ

and 198 Sixth Avenue, New York
NY10013

British Library Cataloguing in Publication Data

Sidney, *Sir* Philip
    Selected writings.
    I. Title   II. Dutton, Richard
    828'.309   PR2341

    ISBN 0-85635-625-5

The publisher acknowledges financial assistance
from the Arts Council of Great Britain

Typeset in 10pt Palatino by Bryan Williamson, Manchester
Printed in England by SRP Ltd, Exeter

Contents

Introduction 7
A Note on the Texts 24
Further Reading 27

Astrophil and Stella 29
The Defence of Poesy 102
Miscellaneous Poems 149

Notes 169

Introduction

You will probably be familiar, at least in outline, with the following account of how Philip Sidney left the battlefield at Zutphen, having received what was to prove a fatal wound, his leg shattered by a musket ball,

> being thirsty with excess of bleeding, he called for drink, which was presently brought to him; but as he was putting the bottle to his mouth, he saw a poor soldier carried along who had eaten his last at the same feast, ghastly casting up his eyes at the bottle. Which Sir Philip perceiving, took it from his head, before he drank, and delivered it to the poor man, with these words, "Thy necessity is yet greater than mine." And when he had pledged this poor soldier, he was presently carried to Arnhem.
>
> – *Life of Sir Philip Sidney*, pp.129-30

There, in the twenty-six days that remained to him, he set about the business of dying as a Christian gentleman should, summoning a number of preachers to him:

> he entreated this choir of divine philosophers about him, to deliver the opinion of the ancient heathen touching the immortality of the soul; first to see what true knowledge she retains of her own essence, out of the light of herself; then to parallel with it the most pregnant authorities of the Old and New Testament, as supernatural revelations, sealed up from our flesh for the divine light of faith to reveal, and work by. Not that he wanted instruction or assurance; but because this fixing of a lover's thoughts upon those eternal beauties, was not only a cheering up of his decaying spirits, but as it were a taking possession of that immortal inheritance that was given unto him by his brotherhood in Christ.
>
> – *Life*, p.137

This serenity persisted to the day of his death, when he showed great fortitude, though his younger brother, Robert, shed "an abundance of tears". At the end, he could neither speak nor open his eyes, but had his hands together on his chest to prove that he was still praying inwardly. It was, we may say, a model death.

A more cynical age may wonder whether it was really like that, and there is certainly some room for scepticism. This account of Sidney's death was written by Fulke Greville, a close friend of Sidney from their days together at Shrewsbury School. (I have somewhat modernised the edition cited in the Further Reading). Greville was not in the Low Countries at the time of Sidney's death and so must have reconstructed events from the accounts of those who were. Moreover, he did not commit them to paper until some twenty-five years later c.1610-11, when he wrote what has come to be known, somewhat erroneously, as his *Life of Sir Philip Sidney*. The *Life* was not published until 1652, long after Greville's own death, for the very good reason that it would deeply have offended either of the Stuart monarchs on the throne in the intervening period. For Greville's biography of his old friend forms part of a nostalgic and idealized evocation of Queen Elizabeth's reign, which implicitly criticizes the far less decorous state of affairs under James I, who was king when it was written. His portrait of Sidney is the centre-piece of a golden vision, and as such it inevitably took on some gilding itself. Greville did not create what we may call the Sidney myth; it began in Sidney's own lifetime or at least very shortly after his death. But his *Life* has helped to perpetuate it.

We may compare Greville's account of the death with an altogether less seemly version recorded by John Aubrey, an inveterate purveyor of tittle-tattle, much of it scurrilous:

He married the daughter of Sir Francis Walsingham, Principal Secretary of Estate (I think his only child) whom he loved very well: in so much that having received some shot or wound in the wars of the Low Countries... he would not (contrary to the injunction of his physicians and surgeons) forbear his carnal knowledge of her, which cost him his life; upon which occasion there were some roguish verses made.

This was written some hundred years after Sidney's death and on no established authority; but Aubrey is right about the identity of Sidney's wife, and it is true that she was with Sidney (in an

8

advanced state of pregnancy) during his last days, something not mentioned by Greville. Clearly Greville's version is the more fitting end of the courtier, soldier, scholar, the paragon of Elizabeth I's Court. But Aubrey's anecdote, whether true or not, tells us something important about the Sidney myth: the man in it is too good for his world; it is only too tempting to believe the most salacious of stories about him, if only to confirm his humanity. There is something of this, I suspect, in Ben Jonson's telling William Drummond of Hawthornden that, "Sir P. Sidney was no pleasant man in countenance, his face being spoiled with pimples, and of high blood and young" – a legacy of measles and smallpox when a child. Jonson's own poetry bears ample testimony to his admiration for Sidney but it was perhaps reassuring to know that the stuff of legend had some blemish, some touch of the ordinary. Even for his near contemporaries, then, the Sidney myth could be hard to swallow. Today, the chief danger is that it distorts our understanding of the man and his times and so makes more difficult a proper appreciation of his writings.

When Sidney died, those who mourned him did so as a hero of Protestant Europe, a model of Christian virtue, of the Renaissance scholar-poet, of the true knight. There is no doubt that Sidney aspired to be seen as all of these, but it may be stretching the truth to say that he really achieved them all within his thirty-two years (1554-86). As a diplomat, he had never been called upon for anything more significant than to make two unremarkable embassies to the continent and to attend upon a number of visiting dignitaries; the campaign in which he died was his first taste of military action. It is true that he had written the first Elizabethan sonnet-sequence in *Astrophil and Stella*, the first significant literary-critical treatise in English in the *Defence of Poesy*, and, in *Arcadia*, what proved to be the most popular prose romance of the age. But Sidney himself, and those who mourned him, would probably have seen his writings as the least of his accomplishments (on his death-bed, he ordered the *Arcadia* to be destroyed) and, being as yet unpublished, they were only known to a close circle of acquaintances.

It is a measure of the difference between what he aspired to be and what he actually achieved in his lifetime that even his knighthood was a touch bogus, coming about as the result of a technicality. The Queen awarded the Order of the Garter to Prince Casimir of the Palatinate, one of the leading Protestant statesmen in Europe. He was unable to attend the installation, in 1583, and so nominated Sidney, whom he had first met on one of the latter's European embassies, to act as proxy for him. Under the rules of the Garter even a proxy had to be of knightly rank and so it was that Philip Sidney received the accolade from the Queen who rarely employed, and perhaps never really appreciated, his talents. As Greville commented, "he never was magistrate nor possessed of any fit stage for eminence to act upon".

The explanation of all these anomalies in Sidney's career and reputation lies less in the man himself than in the role in life to which he was born. On his father's side, he belonged to a family which, like the Cecils and the Bacons, had risen to prominence in the service of the Tudors. His father, Sir Henry, became President of the Marches of Wales early in Elizabeth's reign, and later was one of the more successful Lord Deputies of Ireland of that era. But on his mother's side, he was born to more stirring and dangerous prospects; Mary Sidney was a Dudley, daughter of John Dudley, Duke of Northumberland, who, with his eldest son, Gilbert, had been executed for trying to place Lady Jane Grey on the throne in place of Queen Mary. Her two surviving brothers, Robert and Ambrose, were, as respectively the Earls of Leicester and of Warwick, two of the most powerful men in Elizabeth's Court. Leicester, in particular, was (in all probability) the one man the Queen ever loved and certainly the only Englishman she seriously considered marrying. Philip Sidney grew up in the shadow of his two great uncles and, until only a few years before his death, seemed destined to be the heir of one or both of them. It was this, long before his own talents had a chance to manifest themselves, that gave Sidney the spotlight of national, and indeed European, attention.

One of the most ironic events of Sidney's life was also one of the earliest: his christening. He was named after one of his godfathers, Philip of Spain, who was married to Queen Mary. As Philip II of Spain he above all others was to advance the Roman Catholic Counter-Reformation against the forces of Protestant

Europe, culminating (as far as England was concerned) in the Spanish Armada of 1588. The irony is that this man came to represent for Sidney *the* enemy, the embodiment of militant Catholicism just as he himself sought to be the embodiment of militant Protestantism; Sidney was to give his life in the fight against him – following his uncle, Leicester, who was by then acknowledged leader of the faction at Court which stood for war with Spain. So much of Sidney's life seems in retrospect pre-determined by the times and position into which he was born. One wonders what it must have meant to him to carry the name and baptismal blessing of his fated enemy with him through life. Certainly it is clear from *Astrophil and Stella* (e.g. the title itself; Sonnet 83) that he was very self-conscious of his name.

Philip Sidney was educated at Shrewsbury School, not far from Ludlow, his father's official residence as Lord President of the Marches of Wales, and at Christ Church, Oxford (1568-71). From an early age he seems to have struck his father as somewhat over-serious and over-studious, and it may have been with the intention of broadening his horizons that Sir Henry took the earliest opportunity of attaching him to a diplomatic mission, which was perhaps the safest way of travelling in Europe at a time of so much religious unrest. He accompanied the Earl of Lincoln to Paris in 1572 for the ratification of the Treaty of Blois, and there met some leading European Protestants, including King Henri of Navarre (later Henri IV of France), the philosopher Ramus and, probably, the Burgundian scholar/statesman Hubert Languet (see p.153), who for some time after this sought not only to be Sidney's friend but also something of a guide and tutor. Languet in particular saw the need for a league of Protestant states to resist the Catholic Counter-Reformation and may have convinced Sidney of this. On the other hand, what both of them saw in Paris that August may have been sufficient argument in itself.

On St Bartholomew's Day (the 24th) mobs incited by an extreme Catholic faction (the Guise party) massacred several thousand Huguenots, the French Protestants. Among those who died were their political leader, Admiral Coligny, and Ramus. Sidney him-self was apparently in no immediate danger, though he moved

11

into the English embassy for added protection. The English ambassador was Francis Walsingham, who was shortly to become Elizabeth's Principal Secretary of State and perhaps the most militantly anti-Catholic of her advisers. Eleven years later, he became Sidney's father-in-law. What they both saw of the St Bartholomew's Day Massacre must have helped to confirm their Protestant convictions.

Sidney remained on the Continent until 1575, visiting many cities in Germany, Switzerland, Italy and Austria and building up an extensive range of contacts with intellectuals and politicians. Two memories of all this travelling found their way into *The Defence of Poesy*: an excursion into Hungary, August-October 1573 (see p.125), and a stay in Vienna, centre of the Holy Roman Empire, autumn-winter 1574-75 (see p.102). Then he returned home in some haste, perhaps because his help and advice were required by the Earl of Leicester for his sumptuous entertainment of the Queen at his Warwickshire seat, Kenilworth. We do not know what part Sidney took in these lavish and legendary celebrations, which lasted from July 9-27th, but he and his parents were present throughout, and it is possible that his knowledge of fashionable Continental practices might be useful: such events in the Renaissance always had a significant political dimension to them.

When the Royal Progress moved on from Kenilworth to neighbouring Chartley House, Sidney was introduced to a family that was to have a marked effect on his fortunes. The head of the family, Walter Devereux, newly created Earl of Essex, was on active service in Ireland. His wife, formerly Lettice Knollys and a cousin of the Queen, was already engaged in a secret affair with the Earl of Leicester; (this culminated in Leicester's second marriage, the Queen's unbridled fury and a Dudley heir who significantly diminished Sidney's prospects). Their daughter, Penelope, then thirteen, was a blonde beauty who was later to acquire some notoriety and to be the Stella of *Astrophil and Stella*. We cannot be sure if they actually met on this occasion, though they had probably met within a year or so when their fathers were negotiating a possible marriage between them (the Earl, who died in September 1576, made it his death-bed wish). That

12

Sidney himself was not anxious for the match may be deduced from Sonnet 33 of *Astrophil and Stella*, where he recalls how "then [I] would not, or could not see my bliss". In the end, like an earlier dynastic proposal that he should marry Anne, daughter of Sir William Cecil (later Lord Burghley, perhaps the most trusted of Elizabeth's advisers), it came to nothing. We do not know either if Sidney met the eight-year old Robert Devereux, who as the second Earl of Essex in some ways modelled himself on Sidney, was bequeathed his best sword and married his widow. He, of course, was Elizabeth's last and tragically troublesome favourite.

Sidney received his first minor Court office as cup-bearer to the Queen, and spent some months in Ireland helping his father, before in 1577 receiving a commission to head an embassy which would tour Europe to explore the possibility of some form of Protestant League. It seems clear that he and his colleagues were to investigate and report; they had no authority to negotiate – the Queen and some of her more wary advisers, like Cecil, were far from convinced that such a League was desirable, since it would inevitably lead to war with Spain. In the event, Sidney had to report that prospects for the League were not good, though he personally struck up a good relationship with the man Protestant Europe looked to as its hero, William of Orange, known as William the Silent, leader of the Protestants in the Low Countries who were struggling to free themselves from their Spanish masters. In fact, William offered Sidney the hand of his beloved elder daughter, Marie of Nassau, in marriage; it would have made him Lord of Holland and Zealand, effectively a prince.

But it would also (as William clearly expected) have drawn the Dudleys, and so potentially England itself, into the struggle against Spain, something Elizabeth was determined to resist. She had also lost faith in Sir Henry Sidney's efforts in Ireland and perhaps suspected Sidney's own ambitions (all dynastic developments at the time had to be seen against the fact that the Queen was still unmarried and it was far from clear who would succeed her). So the months dragged on, and finally the proposal came to nothing. At twenty-three, Sidney had been the centre of European attention. But his prospects would never look as bright again, nor would the Queen ever use him again in any major

13

capacity.

Sidney had been living like a Dudley without the resources or official position to support him, and he slipped into debts from which he never recovered. He invested in Frobisher's expeditions to the Americas but without the return he had hoped for; he came increasingly to see America and its gold as the crucial battleground in the fight against Spain, a political conviction reflected in Richard Hakluyt's dedication to him of his *Divers Voyages touching the Discovery of America* (1582), a work of Protestant propaganda as much as history or geography. It also seems to have been in the period of frustration after his European embassy that he first took a serious interest in writing, probably in the prolonged visits he made to his sister Mary, who was now married to the Earl of Pembroke and living at his country estate, Wilton in Wiltshire.

The work that most preoccupied him in these retreats from Court and political life was the *Arcadia*, a long prose romance interspersed with verse passages. When it was published, after his death, it was prefaced with a letter he had written to Mary in connection with its composition:

> Here now have you (most dear, and most worthy to be dear lady) this idle work of mine, which, I fear, like the spider's web, will be thought fitter to be swept away than worn to any other purpose. For my own part, in very truth...I could well find in my heart to cast out in some desert of forgetfulness this child which I am loath to father...Your dear self can best witness the manner [of composition] , being done in loose sheets of paper, most of it in your presence; the rest by sheets sent unto you as fast as they were done...Read it, then, at your idle times, and the follies your good judgement will find in it blame not, but laugh at. And so, looking for no better stuff than as in a haberdasher's shop, glasses or feathers, you will continue to love the writer, who doth exceedingly love you...

This is revealing, but we must beware of taking it too much at face value. Sidney may talk of an "idle work" for "idle times" but it is difficult to dismiss anything that runs to eight hundred pages of modern print as exactly trivial. And it is now clear from what

14

we know of the state of the text that, having finished one version of the book (the *Old Arcadia*, c.1578-80), he began a thorough revision (the *New Arcadia*, probably after 1584), which does not exactly square with his talk of it as a careless trifle. The fact is that here, as elsewhere, Sidney is invoking the *sprezzatura* tradition of authorship espoused by most Renaissance courtiers, playing down the craftsmanship, scholarship and seriousness of anything written by a gentleman. The same tradition frowns on publication, preferring select distribution in manuscript among a judging few to the vulgar professionalism of print. In its way, the whole tradition is a form of conceit, an assumption of natural superiority, compounded by the determination to succeed without apparent effort. We should not let the fact that Sidney did not commit any of his own works to print lead us to conclude that he really felt they were "idle". In as much as Sidney seemed to subscribe to such a view he was himself helping to create the Sidney "myth". We should particularly bear this whole *sprezzatura* manuscript tradition in mind when trying to take a balanced view of the allusive knowingness of *Astrophil and Stella*, pre-eminently a work written for a judging few.

So writing was important to Sidney, partly as a fitting accomplishment for the rounded Renaissance aristocrat he strove to be, but also as a constructive respite from the frustrations of his public life. The tensions of these perhaps surface in a remarkably blunt note he wrote in 1578 to his father's secretary, Molyneux, whom he suspected of tampering with his correspondence. It concludes: "if ever I know you do so much as read any letter I write to my father without his commandment or my consent, I will thrust my dagger into you. And trust to it, for I speak it in earnest. In the meantime, farewell." Greville's paragon clearly had an explosive temper, though perhaps with his ultra-civilized manners he kept it better in check than many of his contemporaries. Nevertheless, his frustrations continued and were underlined that same year in the Queen's response to *The Lady of May*, a pastoral entertainment he wrote for her visit to Wanstead, Leicester's estate near Greenwich. It took the form of a debate between a forester, an active man, and a shepherd, a contemplative one, about the merits of their respective life-styles; as was usual, it was left to the Queen to render a final verdict. It is clear that Sidney wanted and expected the forester to win, probably because his active life represented – in a suitably coded form – the militant Protestant policies for which Leicester and Sidney stood, while the shepherd represented the circumspect policies of such as Burghley. Whether because the Queen had not followed the implications of the piece or, more likely, because she had followed them only too well, the Queen favoured the shepherd.

These tensions took a more serious turn the following year, when it seemed likely that the Queen was going to marry the Duke of Alençon, brother of the French king. Burghley backed the marriage, seeing a French alliance as the most diplomatic way of keeping Spain at bay; Walsingham and Leicester opposed it, as pre-empting more militant policies. Alençon's agents in England adroitly chose this time to reveal to the Queen that Leicester was now secretly married to her cousin, the Countess of Essex, and her fury knew no bounds. The tension between the two factions at Court boiled over that summer in a furious row over the use of a tennis court, between the Earl of Oxford, Burghley's son-in-law, and Sidney, who naturally supported his uncle. The Queen was angry that two of her courtiers should have behaved, as she saw it, in a way that reflected credit on neither of them; and she made a point of reminding Sidney that he was still a commoner, while Oxford was the seventeenth de Vere of that title. Sidney responded with a long and forceful letter to her, outlining objections to the French marriage. She let it be known that he was no longer welcome at Court.

So Sidney retired to Wilton once more, and literature again became central to his life. This is the period when he was associated with the "Areopagus", a circle of poets including his friends Edward Dyer and Fulke Greville, and Edmund Spenser who was then attached to Leicester's household and had dedicated his *Shepherds' Calendar* (1579) to Sidney. (See *The Defence of Poesy*, p.139). They discussed such matters as the reform of English poetry, the use of classical metre in English verse, the possibility of integrating poetry and music, and the moral significance of literature – which must always have been a central issue since the moral influence of literature was the chief accepted justification for its existence. It must have been in this context that Sidney composed *The Defence of Poesy*, the first substantial critical treatise in English.

A long-standing tradition, which has recently been challenged, has it that Sidney wrote the *Defence* to refute some of the opinions expressed in a book dedicated to him, Stephen Gosson's *The School of Abuse* (1579); this was a Puritan work that attacked aspects of poetry and other contemporary arts. Whether or not Gosson's book occasioned the *Defence*, its existence helps us to put that work in context. Sidney belonged politically to the militant Protestant faction at Court, and his personal faith had a definite Calvinist complexion. It is not improbable that someone like Gosson, who did not know him personally, might conclude that his convictions were uniformly Puritan and extended to a repudiation of literature and drama as licentious distractions from God's truth. But Sidney, like Spenser and, later, Milton, was as much a humanist as a Puritan (a term often used far too loosely): literature had a place as long as it was used to inculcate virtue, to help Christian men rise above the chaos of sin and confusion into which they were born. When Sidney uses the term "poetry" (or "poesy" – the terms are virtually synonymous, though Sidney uses the latter specifically to denot the art or faculty of writing poetry), he does not simply mean verse, but any literature with this moral, indeed inspirational purpose. Wherever we look in the *Defence*, whether he is discussing the style, or the genre, or the subject-matter of literature, it is its functional quality, its capacity to change men's behaviour for the better which is of paramount importance to him – and the basis of his claim that it is superior to all other intellectual pursuits, notably philosophy and history, with the single and over-riding exception of divinity. Viewed in this light, we can see that the *Defence of Poesy* – with its casual references to Sidney's diplomatic and courtly accomplishments, its forensic rhetoric graced with a lively and informal style, its solid scholarship all but hidden behind gentlemanly self-depreciation – is of a piece with his public career.

At the New Year 1581 Sidney made his peace with the Queen, presenting her with a jewel-encrusted whip by which he symbolically submitted to her will. But, though he became a Member of

17

Parliament and helped in the entertainment of Don Antonio, the pretender to the Portuguese crown, no significant office or reward came his way. That Whitsun he and Greville took part in the tournament of the Fortress of Perfect Beauty, one of the most splendid of the pseudo-medieval chivalric exercises which were a regular feature of the Elizabethan Court. This may be the one he mentions in *Astrophil and Stella*, since French commissioners were certainly there to see him:

> Having this day my horse, my hand, my lance
> Guided so well, that I obtain'd the prize,
> Both by the judgement of the English eyes,
> And of some sent from that sweet enemy France...
>
> (Sonnet 41)

But Sidney would have to pay for all the resplendent armour and finery of the occasion himself, an expensive way of staying in the Queen's eye (or Stella's), particularly since he was now no longer the principal heir-apparent of the Dudleys.

The general lowering of his condition and expectations may explain why, in September 1583, he married Frances Walsingham, the daughter of his old friend and ally. In political terms it had the advantage of cementing the relationship between the Dudleys and the Queen's Principal Secretary, but it was not as splendid a match as Penelope Devereux, much less Marie de Nassau, would have been. Moreover, the Queen disapproved of the match, which was a high price to pay. But Walsingham paid off £1500 of Sidney's debts and saved the couple considerable expense by taking them into his own house.

The marriage inevitably brings us to the great enigma of Sidney's life, the circumstances behind his writing of *Astrophil and Stella*. It is beyond question that the characters, Astro-Phil (Star-Lover) and Stella (Star) represent in some wise Sidney himself and Penelope Devereux. In the sequence, Sidney includes a number of autobiographical details, such as references to his father's duties in Ireland (Sonnet 30), and he puns several times on Penelope's married name, which was Rich (e.g. Sonnets 24 and 37); moreover, several contemporaries readily made these identifications. What we cannot know is the precise relationship

18

that lay behind the writing of the poems. They must have been written after November 1581, when Penelope married Lord Rich, since throughout the sequence Stella's married status is one of the frustrations Astrophil has to bear; he regrets that he paid no attention to her before this crucial impediment. Such details as the European crises listed in Sonnet 30 (Turkish threats to Spain, Maximilian II's invasion of Muscovy etc.) point to the summer of 1582, while nothing definitely points to any date later than 1583. It would be reasonable, then, to suppose that the poems belong to a period, perhaps no more than a year in length, shortly before Sidney's marriage. But this takes us no closer to knowing whether they record an actual liaison between Sidney and a married woman. We know that Sidney was no saint, while Penelope Devereux was as hot-headed and unconventional as her brother, the Earl of Essex; whatever her relations with Sidney, it is clear there was never any love lost between her and her husband, whom she eventually divorced – but not before bearing several children to her lover, Sir Charles Blount (Lord Mountjoy). Perhaps the most telling piece of evidence, assuming we can believe it, is from an account of Sidney's death-bed confession recorded by George Gifford, one of the divines who attended him in his final illness: "There came to my remembrance a vanity wherein I had taken delight, whereof I had not rid myself. It was my Lady Rich. But I rid myself of it, and presently my joy and comfort returned within a few hours".

Such death-bed "confessions" are notoriously unreliable, and anyway it is not clear whether adultery itself or merely the thought of it was the "vanity" that troubled him. We will probably never know the biographical truth. To those who will suppose that great love-poetry must arise from actual experience of the emotions involved, we may oppose the opinion of no less an expert than John Donne (who clearly learned a lot from Sidney), when he insisted that his own love poems were most successful when "there was least of truth in them"; that is, when they were based on fictitious situations. When Thomas Nashe wrote a preface for one of the earliest printed editions of these poems, he described *Astrophil and Stella* as a fiction portraying "the tragi-comedy of love...the argument cruel chastity, the prologue hope, the epilogue despair". This underplays the teasing, game-playing element that must have been present, particularly for the original manuscript readers (see, for example, Sonnet 104; Sidney really did have stars on his armour, as in l.10, and tantalises us throughout about the possibilities of "hid meaning", l.12) but it is a fair description of the *literary* experience that the sequence offers us, and which now is or should be our prime concern.

The fact is that the "plot" of a would-be adulterous relationship allows Sidney's poetry to explore precisely the themes and emotions that, from his other works, we should expect to interest him: hope, despair, idealism, cynicism, reason, passion, virtue, corruption. It is the opposition and frequently irreconcilable contradictions between these themes that underlie the "problems old" of which Sidney talks in Sonnet 3 (l.6) – problems here in the old sense of "a question proposed for academic discussion or scholastic disputation" (OED). In the *Defence* Sidney defends the lyric poet on the grounds that he "gives moral precepts, and natural problems" (p.124) and later categorizes the form his own sonnet-sequence was to take as "that lyrical kind of songs and sonnets" (p.143). Unfortunately, he never explains how his readers might engage with those "problems" (his usual model is epic or heroic poetry, where things are obviously very different) and so presumably obtain moral benefit.

Astrophil's attempts to come to terms with the conflicting pressures that assail him – finally having all hopes dashed when passion gets the better of him – are a sustained lesson in self-knowledge and self-deception, which hangs (in my view) on an ironic distance between Astrophil and his alter-ego, Sidney. Take Sonnet 52 as a typical example: it is a traditional Petrarchan sonnet in its weighing of conflicting interests and emotions, conducted as if it were a legal debate. Man is ambivalently torn between the instinct of his divine soul to rise towards the perfection which it recognizes in Stella's Virtue and the inclination of his physical passions towards her carnal attributes (an attraction which Astrophil always modestly but ambiguously calls Love). The resolution of the conflict, which Astrophil pronounces, is a judgement of Solomon: Virtue may have Stella's soul, so long as Love can have her body. But a moment's reflection – called for by the poet Sidney and patently not by his "mouthpiece", Astrophil – tells us that this is an impossibility. We cannot (at least in a Christian universe) divorce our care for our immortal souls from what we do with our bodies. The neat resolution of the conflict, mirrored in the neat rounding-off of the fourteen-line structure, is a sham, an artifice, a challenge to the reader to reconsider first principles. This is essentially what Sidney does from the beginning, where the triumphant solution to Sonnet 1 – "Fool", said my Muse to me, "look in thy heart and write" – is a paradoxical negation of its own sentiments: it is art concealing art, a long way removed from the casual inspiration which it seems to advocate. Sidney the artist is always looking quizzically over his creations' shoulders and at the reader.

In the past critics have often resisted coming to this conclusion about *Astrophil and Stella* (as they have about much Renaissance love poetry) for fear that it should seem to imply that the poems are *only* exercises in technique, demonstrations of verbal and rhetorical skills – the antithesis of what we post-Romantics have come to value in poetry. The fact that these poets did imitate and echo each other, and their predecessors, so extensively already made them suspect. But surely our own generation, which has seen in the novel the pyrotechnical game-playing of Nabokov, Borges, Barth, Fowles, Lodge, Eco and many others, is well placed to appreciate the kinds of excitement, involvement, and indeed sincerity, which are possible within this kind of literary "game-playing". And if we appreciate that, we will be better placed to understand how the Sidney who, in *The Defence of Poesy*, argues that true poetry "doth intend the winning of the mind from wickedness to virtue", could write a sequence of poems about a would-be adulterous relationship.

Writing of other people's efforts, he complains: "But truly many of such writings, as come under the banner of unresistible love, if I were a mistress, would never persuade me they were in love." In attempting to improve on them, of course, he introduced elements of colloquial conviction, psychological realism, personal drama. But credibility is never merely an end in itself; the more we understand Astrophil and appreciate his dilemmas – the more, paradoxically, that we are convinced that he *is* Sidney –

the greater should be our awareness of his failings, his self-centredness, his moral short-sightedness. Whatever the auto-biographical basis of these poems, they are very much about the "self", that reliably unreliable entity which has been so central to literature from the Renaissance onwards. And while the *Defence* never discusses the kind of dialectical process between the text and the reader towards a kind of virtuous understanding that I am suggesting (it talks rather simply of the reader being attracted towards virtue and repelled by vice) this examination of the morally unregenerate "self" in *Astrophil and Stella* is perfectly consonant with the central tenets of the critical treatise.

By the time of his marriage, however, and although he probably continued to revise the *Arcadia*, literature must once more have been relegated behind public affairs in his attention. The situation in the Low Countries was becoming critical as the Spanish seemed to be winning; then William of Orange was assassinated, and Elizabeth finally decided, in 1585, that direct English intervention was unavoidable. Leicester was to be commander-in-chief of the English troops and Sidney was to be governor of the forces at Flushing – a key position, since it controlled traffic in and out of Antwerp, effectively second in command. Ironically, by now Sidney was convinced that the Americas rather than the Low Countries was where Spain should be fought, and he had set up a secret privateering expedition with Sir Francis Drake, which he was more keen to pursue than this new commission. But Drake became nervous about taking him, and the Queen intervened sternly to order him not to go – so the Sidney legend was to be of the battlefield martyr rather than one of the famous generation of "sea dogs".

Sidney made some positive contributions to the campaign, including the capture of the walled city of Axel without the loss of a man. But the whole expedition was bedevilled with problems, not least because Leicester was an ineffective and tactless commander. When, against Elizabeth's express orders, he accepted the Dutch offer of the post of Governor-General – in effect sovereign of the Netherlands – he lost all hope of steady support from home. So Sidney died in a muddled, inglorious campaign that was not of his own choosing. But the timing was fortuitous.

It was already apparent that this was the prelude to a more openly national struggle. Philip II of Spain noted briefly on the despatch that told him of Sidney's death, "He was my godson", already involved in preparations for the Spanish Armada that sailed less than two years later. In this climate, the Sidney legend took root quickly, with some help from Walsingham, who paid for a funeral on a princely scale in old St Paul's. By a final irony, the man himself was translated in the way he had described poets as translating reality: "Nature never set forth the earth in so rich tapestry, as divers poets have done, . . . Her world is brazen, the poets only deliver a golden". The golden Sidney – stripped of life's frustrations and disappointments, his short temper, his debts and possible adultery – was a model to the generations that followed.

A Note on the Texts

For reasons already explained, Sidney published none of his works in his own lifetime. In respect of both *Astrophil and Stella* and *The Defence of Poesy* the absence of the poet's own authority from the early editions poses some problems for the modern editor, but none of a major nature.

Astrophil and Stella was first published in 1591 in two quarto editions which appear to have had no sanction from any of Sidney's family or friends. I have followed recent editorial practice in preferring the text given in the 1598 Folio of Sidney's works, which there is good reason for supposing was supervised by his sister, Mary, Countess of Pembroke. It is the fullest of the early texts and includes the songs as they are given here (some texts have none, others only some), lyric embellishments on the narrative running through the sonnets. I have consulted a number of modern editions of the work, including W.A. Ringler's standard *The Poems of Sir Philip Sidney* (Oxford, 1962) and David Kalstone's *The Selected Poetry and Prose of Sir Philip Sidney* (New York and London, 1970). I am indebted to them for numerous readings and notes. To Ringler in particular I owe sanction for the version of the title as it is used in this edition; the early texts, including the 1598 Folio, give it as *Astrophel and Stella*. But "Astrophel" is meaningless as a name, while Sidney appears to want to play on his own name, as he does ("Philisides") in the *Old Arcadia*. Professor Ringler argues the case, convincingly to my mind, on p.458.

What I have called *The Defence of Poesy* was first published in two independent texts in 1595, one with the title *An Apology for Poetry*, the other *The Defence of Poesy*. There is no way of knowing which, if either, was Sidney's title. Both pose problems for modern readers, since the work is not an "apology" in the modern sense, though it *is* an *apologia*, a defence or vindication; and "poesy" is an outdated term with quaint associations. There is a recent tendency by scholars to cut the Gordian knot and call it *The Defence of Poetry*, but that is unfortunate because there already is another major critical treatise, Shelley's *A Defence of Poetry*, with which it may be confused. I have opted for *The Defence of Poesy* mainly because "defence" needs no glossing, while "poesy" may be useful in reminding readers that Sidney's definition of poetry/poesy was very different from the one (literature in verse) commonly used today.

I do not mean to imply, however, in that choice of title, that this is specifically an edition of the 1595 *Defence*. The two 1595 texts are very similar in essentials and neither is obviously superior to the other. There are good modern editions of both texts: the *Defence* is included in the standard edition of *The Complete Works of Sir Philip Sidney*, ed. A. Feuillerat, 4 vols. (Cambridge, 1912-26), while the *Apology* is the basis of the best scholarly edition of the treatise, by Geoffrey Shepherd (London, 1965). I have consulted both editions and am indebted to Professor Shepherd, in particular, in my notes. I have operated on the assumption that what is needed is not, therefore, another text for scholars but one for interested modern readers. On that basis I have conflated the early texts liberally, always opting – where there is a choice – for the version which will be more accessible to the modern reader. An obvious example is the use of "s" against "eth" as the end of 3rd person singular verbs; the 1595 texts are quite eclectic about this, but I have used the modern "s" wherever one or the other sanctions it. I have not burdened the text with an editorial apparatus but wish to make plain that, while this is not a redaction of a particular early text, all my readings (except where specifically noted) are based on one early text or another.

The Miscellaneous Poems included here are all either from the *Arcadia* or from *Certain Sonnets*. Within the space available, I have tried to give an indication of the range, quality and originality of Sidney's poetry outside *Astrophil and Stella*, which is his most substantial single achievement in verse. The *Arcadia*, as I have mentioned, was revised by Sidney himself and then again by his editors after his death. I have tried to indicate in the notes the derivation of the individual pieces; where I have referred simply to the *Arcadia*, rather than to the Old or New form I have in mind the Penguin edition by Maurice Evans cited in the Further Reading, which gives a modernized version of the text as it was known to most Elizabethan readers. Most of these poems, though they read adequately by themselves, take on added dimensions in the contexts Sidney (or his early editors) devised for them; many of

25

them are, as it were, lyric meditations on particular moments or states of mind. Again, I have tried to give sufficient information about these contexts in the notes, but the interested reader should follow up by looking at a text of the *Arcadia* itself. *Certain Sonnets* (sonnet in the sense of lyric, though some pieces are in the form we now associate with the term) is an early collection, apparently put together by Sidney himself, though not published until 1598; there is no narrative thread running through the collection, as there is with *Astrophil and Stella*, but the arrangement does seem deliberate, culminating in two sonnets (printed here as MP 10 and 11) which, in renouncing desire and love, virtually renounce poetry as well. Fortunately, they only represent a passing mood for Sidney, but they make a fitting conclusion to this selection.

I have modernized the spelling of all these works, including the usual normalization of "i", "j", "u" and "v". The only exceptions are that, in the poems, I have retained contractions (some odd to modern ears and eyes) where they are necessary for the rhythm, including past participles ending in "t" (maskt, matcht etc.); I have also retained occasional old spelling essential for a rhyme. Renaissance punctuation works on very different principles (mainly oratorical ones) from those that apply today. In the *Defence* I have modernized liberally, to try to convey the sense as clearly as possible. In the poetry, however, I have been much more restrained, on the grounds that the poetry is richer for nuances and associations which regularized modern punctuation might tend to obscure. I have tried to make it a rule only to intervene where I think that there is a serious risk that a modern reader might get lost or confused. If the lightness of punctuation poses problems for a reader in Sidney's more complex periods, I would always recommend reading the passage out loud (as Sidney's contemporaries probably did). The sense is usually clear enough once you have determined the rhythm.

I have provided a minimum of annotation to help the modern reader through these works. Wherever possible I have included glosses in or adjacent to the relevant passages, alerting readers of the poetry with a † in the text. But when a note might unduly clutter the text, I have removed it to the Notes at the end, alerting readers with a *.

Further Reading

Editions:

The Complete Works of Sir Philip Sidney. Albert Feuillerat (ed.) 4 vols. (Cambridge, 1912-26). The *Prose Works* were reissued separately, in 4 volumes, in 1962.

The Poems of Sir Philip Sidney. W.A. Ringler (ed.) (Oxford, 1962)

An Apology for Poetry. Geoffrey Shepherd (ed.) (London, 1965)

Miscellaneous Prose of Sir Philip Sidney. K. Duncan-Jones and J. Van Dorsten (eds.) (Oxford, 1973)

The Countess of Pembroke's Arcadia. Maurice Evans (ed.) (Harmondsworth, 1977)

The Selected Poetry and Prose of Sir Philip Sidney. David Kalstone (ed.) (New York and London, 1970)

Life and Times

John Buxton, *Sir Philip Sidney and the English Renaissance* (London, 1954)

Fulke Greville, *Life of Sir Philip Sidney*, ed. Nowell Smith (Oxford, 1907)

Roger Howell, *Sir Philip Sidney: the Shepherd Knight* (Boston & Toronto, 1968)

James M. Osborn, *Young Philip Sidney* (New Haven, 1972)

J.A. Van Dorsten, *Poets, Patrons, and Professors: Sir Philip Sidney, Daniel Rogers, and the Leiden Humanists* (Leiden, 1962)

M.W. Wallace, *The Life of Sir Philip Sidney*, (London, 1915)

Criticism

Dorothy Connell, *Sir Philip Sidney: the Maker's Mind* (Oxford, 1977)

A.C. Hamilton, *Sir Philip Sidney: A Study of His Life and Works* (Cambridge, 1977)

David Kalstone, *Sidney's Poetry* (Cambridge, Mass., 1965)

Robert Kimbrough, *Sir Philip Sidney* (1971)

J.W. Lever, *The Elizabethan Love Sonnet* (London, 1956)

Robert L. Montgomery, *Symmetry and Sense: The Poetry of Sir Philip Sidney* (Austin, Texas, 1961)

J.G. Nichols, *The Poetry of Sir Philip Sidney* (Liverpool, 1974)

Neil Rudenstine, *Sidney's Poetic Development* (Cambridge, Mass., 1967)

G.F. Waller and M.D. Moore (eds.), *Sir Philip Sidney and the Interpretation of Renaissance Culture* (London and Totowa, New Jersey, 1984)

John Webster (ed. and trans.), *William Temple's 'Analysis' of Sir Philip Sidney's 'Apology for Poetry'* (Binghampton, New York, 1984)

Andrew D. Weiner, *Sir Philip Sidney and the Poetics of Protestantism* (Minneapolis, 1978)

Richard B. Young, 'English Petrarke: A Study of Sidney's *Astrophil and Stella*' in *Three Studies in the Renaissance: Sidney, Jonson, Milton* (New Haven, 1958)

Astrophil and Stella

1

Loving in truth, and fain in verse my love to show,
That the dear She might take some pleasure of my pain:
Pleasure might cause her read, reading might make her know,
Knowledge might pity win, and pity grace obtain,
   I sought fit words to paint the blackest face of woe,
Studying inventions fine, her wits to entertain:
Oft turning others' leaves, to see if thence would flow
Some fresh and fruitful showers upon my sun-burn'd brain.
   But words came halting forth, wanting Invention's stay,
Invention, Nature's child, fled step-dame Study's blows,
And others' feet[†] still seem'd but strangers in my way.
Thus great with child to speak, and helpless in my throes,
   Biting my truand[†] pen, beating myself for spite,
   "Fool," said my Muse to me, "look in thy heart[†] and write".

feet with sense of poetic feet; *truand* idle; *heart* i.e. at the image of Stella there

2

Not at first sight, nor with a dribbed[†] shot
   Love gave the wound, which while I breathe will bleed:
   But known worth did in mine[†] of time proceed,
Till by degrees it had full conquest got.
I saw and liked, I liked but loved not,
   I loved, but straight did not what Love[†] decreed:
   At length to Love's decrees, I forc'd, agreed,
Yet with repining at so partial[†] lot.
   Now even that footstep of lost liberty
Is gone, and now like slave-born Muscovite,
I call it praise to suffer tyranny;
And now employ the remnant of my wit,
   To make myself believe, that all is well,
   While with a feeling skill I paint my hell.

dribbed random; *mine* as in siege warfare; *Love* almost always, as here, implies
blind, wanton Cupid; *partial* unbalanced, unfair

Let dainty wits cry on the Sisters nine[†],
That bravely maskt[†], their fancies may be told:
Or Pindar's apes[†], flaunt they in phrases fine,
Enam'ling with pied flowers their thoughts of gold:
 Or else let them in statelier glory shine,
Ennobling new found tropes[†] with problems[†] old:
Or with strange similes enrich each line,
Of herbs or beasts, which Ind or Afric hold.
 For me in sooth, no Muse but one I know:
 Phrases and problems from my reach do grow,
And strange things cost too dear for my poor sprites.
 How then? even thus: in Stella's face I read,
 What love and beauty be, then all my deed
But copying is, what in her Nature writes.

Sisters nine the Muses; *bravely maskt* splendidly bedecked/hidden; *Pindar's apes* imitators of Pindar; *tropes* rhetorical figures; *problems* questions for disputation

Virtue alas, now let me take some rest,
Thou setst a bate[†] between my will and wit,
If vain love have my simple soul opprest:
Leave what thou likest not, deal not thou with it.
 Thy sceptre use in some old Cato's[†] breast;
Churches or schools are for thy seat more fit:
I do confess, pardon a fault confest:
My mouth too tender is for thy hard bit.
 But if that needs thou wilt usurping be,
 The little reason that is left in me,
And still th'effect of thy persuasions prove[†]:
 I swear, my heart such one shall show to thee,
 That shrines in flesh so true a deity,
That Virtue, thou thyself shalt be in love.

bate discord; *old Cato* "a bitter punisher of faults"; *prove* try

It is most true, that eyes are form'd to serve
The inward light[†]: and that the heavenly part
Ought to be king, from whose rules who do swerve,
Rebels to Nature, strive for their own smart.
   It is most true, what we call Cupid's dart,
An image is, which for ourselves we carve;
And, fools, adore in temple of our heart,
Till that good god make church and churchman starve.
   True, that true Beauty Virtue is indeed,
Whereof this beauty can be but a shade,
Which elements with mortal mixture breed:
True, that on earth we are but pilgrims made,
   And should in soul up to our country move:
   True, and yet true that I must Stella love.

inward light reason

Some lovers speak when they their Muses entertain,
Of hopes begot by fear, of wot not what desires:
Of force of heav'nly beams, infusing hellish pain:
Of living deaths, dear wounds, fair storms and freezing fires:[†]
   Some one his song in Jove, and Jove's strange tales[†] attires,
Bordered with bulls and swans, powdered with golden rain:
Another humbler wit to shepherd's pipe[†] retires,
Yet hiding royal blood full oft in rural vein.
   To some a sweetest plaint, a sweetest style affords,
   While tears pour out his ink, and sighs breathe out his words:
His paper, pale despair, and pain his pen doth move.
   I can speak what I feel, and feel as much as they,
   But think that all the map of my state I display,
When trembling voice brings forth that I do Stella love.

lines 3 & 4 Petrarchan oxymorons; *Jove's strange tales* Ovidian myths of Jove's loves/rapes; *shepherd's pipe* pastoral love poetry

7

When Nature made her chief work, Stella's eyes,
In colour black, why wrapt she beams so bright?
Would she in beamy[†] black, like painter wise,
Frame daintiest lustre, mixt of shades and light?
   Or did she else that sober hue devise,
In object[†] best to knit and strength our sight,
Lest if no veil these brave gleams did disguise,
They sun-like should more dazzle than delight?
   Or would she her miraculous power show,
That whereas black seems Beauty's contrary,
She even in black doth make all beauties flow?
Both so and thus, she minding Love should be
   Placed ever there, gave him this mourning weed,
   To honour all their deaths, who for her bleed.

beamy radiant; *in object* in order

8

Love born in Greece, of late fled from his native place[†],
   Forc'd by a tedious proof, that Turkish hardened heart,
   Is no fit mark to pierce with his fine pointed dart:
And pleased with our soft peace, stayed here his flying race.
But finding these North climes do coldly him embrace,
   Not used to frozen clips[†], he strave to find some part,
   Where with most ease and warmth he might employ his art:
At length he perch'd himself in Stella's joyful face,
   Whose fair skin, beamy eyes, like morning sun on snow,
Deceiv'd the quaking boy, who thought from so pure light,
Effects of lively heat, must needs in nature grow.
But she most fair, most cold, made him thence take his flight
   To my close[†] heart, where while some firebrands he did lay,
   He burnt unwares his wings, and cannot fly away.

native place Cyprus, captured by the Turks in 1573; *clips* embraces; *close* nearby/
confined/secret

Queen Virtue's court, which some call Stella's face,
  Prepar'd by Nature's chiefest furniture†,
  Hath his front† built of alabaster pure;
Gold is the covering of that stately place.
The door by which sometimes comes forth her grace,
  Red porphyr is, which lock of pearl makes sure:
  Whose porches rich (which names of cheeks endure)
Marble mixt red and white do interlace.
  The windows now through which this heav'nly guest
Looks over the world, and can find nothing such,
Which dare claim from those lights the name of best
Of touch* they are that without touch doth touch,
  Which Cupid's self from Beauty's mine did draw:
  Of touch they are, and poor I am their straw.

furniture furnishing; *front* also face/forehead

10

Reason, in faith thou art well serv'd, that still
Wouldst brabbling† be with sense and love in me:
I rather wish'd thee climb the Muses' hill,
Or reach the fruit of Nature's choicest tree,
  Or seek heav'n's course, or heav'n's inside to see:
Why shouldst thou toil our thorny soil to till?
Leave sense, and those which sense's objects be:
Deal thou with powers of thoughts, leave love to will.
  But thou wouldst needs fight both with love and sense,
With sword of wit, giving wounds of dispraise,
Till down-right blows did foil thy cunning fence†:
For soon as they strake thee with Stella's rays,
  Reason thou kneel'dst, and offeredst straight to prove
  By reason good, good reason her to love.

brabbling quarrelling; *fence* swordsmanship

11

In truth, O Love, with what a boyish kind
    Thou doest proceed in thy most serious ways:
    That when the heav'n to thee his best displays,
Yet of that best thou leav'st the best behind.
For like a child that some fair book doth find,
    With gilded leaves or colour'd vellum plays,
    Or at the most on some fine picture stays,
But never heeds the fruit of writer's mind:
    So when thou saw'st in Nature's cabinet
Stella, thou straight lookst babies in her eyes[†],
In her cheek's pit thou didst thy pitfold[†] set,
And in her breast bopeep[†] or couching lies,
    Playing and shining in each outward part:
    But, fool, seekst not to get into her heart.

lookst babies sees his own reflection; *pitfold* pitfall, trap for birds; *bopeep* as in the teasing child's game

12

Cupid, because thou shin'st in Stella's eyes,
    That from her locks, thy day-nets[†], none scapes free,
    That those lips swell, so full of thee they be,
That her sweet breath makes oft thy flames to rise,
That in her breast thy pap well sugared lies,
    That her grace gracious makes thy wrongs, that she
    What words soe'er she speaks persuades for thee,
That her clear voice lifts thy fame to the skies.
    Thou countest Stella thine, like those whose powers
Having got up a breach by fighting well,
Cry, "Victory, this fair day all is ours."
O no, her heart is such a citadel,
    So fortified with wit, stor'd with disdain,
    That to win it, is all the skill and pain.

day-nets nets with mirrors to catch larks

Phoebus was judge between Jove, Mars, and Love
   Of those three gods, whose arms the fairest were:
   Jove's golden shield did eagle sables[†] bear,
Whose talents[†] held young Ganymede[†] above:
But in vert[†] field Mars bare a golden spear,
   Which through a bleeding heart his point did shove:
   Each had his crest, Mars carried Venus' glove,
Jove on his helm the thunderbolt did rear.
Cupid then smiles, for on his crest there lies
   Stella's fair hair, her face he makes his shield,
   Where roses gules[†] are borne in silver field.
Phoebus drew wide the curtains of the skies
   To blaze[†] these last, and swear devoutly then,
   The first, thus matcht, were scarcely gentlemen.

sables, vert, gules heraldic colours, black, green, red; *talents* talons; *Ganymede* beautiful boy carried off by Jove's eagle to be cupbearer to the gods; *blaze* heraldic display, publish/proclaim

Alas have I not pain enough my friend,
   Upon whose breast a fiercer gripe[†] doth tire[†]
   Than did on him[†] who first stale down the fire,
While Love on me doth all his quiver spend,
But with your rhubarb[†] words you must contend
   To grieve me worse, in saying that desire
   Doth plunge my well-form'd soul even in the mire
Of sinful thoughts, which do in ruin end?
   If that be sin which doth the manners frame,
Well stay'd with truth in word and faith of deed,
Ready of wit and fearing nought but shame:
If that be sin which in fixt hearts doth breed
   A loathing of all loose unchastity,
   Then Love is sin, and let me sinful be.

gripe vulture; *tire* tear with beak; *him* Prometheus; *rhubarb* bitter

15

You that do search for every purling spring,
  Which from the ribs of old Parnassus[†] flows,
  And every flower[†], not sweet perhaps, which grows
Near thereabout, into your poesy[†] wring;
You that do dictionary's method[†] bring
  Into your rhymes, running in rattling rows:
  You that poor Petrarch's long deceased woes,
With new-born sighs and denizen'd[†] wit do sing.
  You take wrong ways, those far-fet helps be such,
  As do bewray a want of inward touch:
And sure at length stol'n goods do come to light.
  But if (both for your love and skill) your name
  You seek to nurse at fullest breasts of Fame,
Stella behold, and then begin to indite[†].

Parnassus home of the Muses; *flower* also, rhetorical figure; *poesy* also, posy;
dictionary's method heavy alliteration; *denizen'd* domesticated; *indite* compose

16

In nature apt to like when I did see
  Beauties, which were of many carats fine,
  My boiling sprites did thither soon incline,
And, Love, I thought that I was full of thee:
But finding not those restless flames in me,
  Which others said did make their souls to pine:
  I thought those babes of some pin's hurt did whine,
By my love judging what Love's pain might be.
  But while I thus with this young lion played,
  Mine eyes (shall I say curst or blest) beheld
Stella; now she is nam'd, need more be said?
In her sight I a lesson new have spell'd,
  I now have learn'd Love right, and learn'd even so,
  As who by being poison'd doth poison know.

His mother† dear Cupid offended late,
  Because that Mars, grown slacker in her love,
  With pricking shot he did not throughly move,
To keep the pace of their first loving state.
The boy refused for fear of Mars's hate,
  Who threaten'd stripes, if he his wrath did prove†:
  But she in chafe him from her lap did shove,
Brake bow, brake shafts, while Cupid weeping sat:
  Till that his grandame Nature pitying it,
Of Stella's brows made him two better bows,
And in her eyes of arrows infinite.
O how for joy he leaps, O how he crows,
  Who straight therewith, like wags new got to play,
  Falls to shrewd† turns, and I was in his way.

mother Venus; *prove* try; *shrewd* naughty

With what sharp checks I in myself am shent†,
  When into Reason's audit I do go:
  And by just counts myself a bankrout know
Of all those goods, which heav'n to me hath lent:
Unable quite to pay even Nature's rent,
  Which unto it by birthright I do owe:
  And which is worse, no good excuse can show,
But that my wealth I have most idly spent.
  My youth doth waste, my knowledge brings forth toys,
My wit doth strive those passions to defend,
Which for reward spoil it with vain annoys.
I see my course to lose myself doth bend:
  I see and yet no greater sorrow take,
  Than that I lose no more for Stella's sake.

shent ashamed

On Cupid's bow how are my heart-strings bent,
   That see my wrack, and yet embrace the same?
   When most I glory, then I feel most shame:
I willing run, yet while I run, repent.
My best wits still their own disgrace invent:
   My very ink turns straight to Stella's name;
   And yet my words, as them my pen doth frame,
Avise themselves that they are vainly spent.
   For though she pass all things, yet what is all
That unto me, who fare like him that both
Looks to the skies, and in a ditch doth fall?
O let me prop my mind, yet in his growth
   And not in Nature for best fruits unfit:
   "Scholar", saith Love, "bend hitherward your wit".

Fly, fly, my friends, I have my death wound; fly,
See there that boy, that murth'ring boy I say,
Who like a thief, hid in dark bush doth lie,
Till bloody bullet get him wrongful prey.
   So tyran he no fitter place could spy,
Nor so fair level† in so secret stay†,
As that sweet black which veils the heav'nly eye:
There himself with his shot he close doth lay.
   Poor passenger†, pass now thereby I did,
And stayed pleas'd with the prospect of the place,
While that black hue from me the bad guest hid:
But straight I saw motions of lightning grace,
   And then descried the glist'ring of his dart:
   But ere I could fly thence, it pierc'd my heart.

level line of fire; *stay* stopping place; *passenger* passer-by

Your words my friend (right healthful caustics) blame
  My young mind marr'd, whom Love doth windlass[†] so,
  That mine own writings like bad servants show
My wits, quick in vain thoughts, in virtue lame:
That Plato I read for nought, but if he tame
  Such coltish gyres[†], that to my birth I owe
  Nobler desires, least else that friendly foe,
Great expectation, wear a train of shame.
  For since mad March great promise made of me,
If now the May of my years much decline,
What can be hoped my harvest time will be?
Sure you say well, your wisdom's golden mine
  Dig deep with learning's spade, now tell me this,
  Hath this world aught so fair as Stella is?

windlass ensnare; *gyres* rapid turnings

In highest way of heav'n the sun did ride,
  Progressing[†] then from fair twins'[†] gold'n place:
  Having no scarf of clouds before his face,
But shining forth of heat in his chief pride;
When some fair ladies, by hard promise tied,
  On horseback met him in his furious race,
  Yet each prepar'd with fan's well-shading grace,
From that foe's wounds their tender skins to hide.
Stella alone with face unarmed march'd,
  Either to do like him, which open shone,
  Or careless of the wealth because her own:
Yet were the hid and meaner beauties parch'd,
  Her daintiest bare went free; the cause was this,
  The sun which others burn'd, did but her kiss.

progressing like royalty; *fair twins* Gemini, in June

23

The curious wits, seeing dull pensiveness
  Bewray itself in my long settled eyes,
  Whence those same fumes of melancholy rise,
With idle pains, and missing aim, do guess.
Some that know how my spring I did address,
  Deem that my Muse some fruit of knowledge plies:
  Others, because the prince my service tries,
Think that I think state errors to redress.
  But harder judges judge ambition's rage,
Scourge of itself, still climbing slipp'ry place,
Holds my young brain captiv'd in golden cage.
O fools, or over-wise, alas the race
  Of all my thoughts hath neither stop nor start,
  But only Stella's eyes and Stella's heart.

24

Rich[†] fools there be, whose base and filthy heart
Lies hatching still the goods wherein they flow:
And damning their own selves to Tantal's smart[†],
Wealth breeding want, more blist, more wretched grow.
  Yet to those fools heav'n such wit doth impart,
As what their hands do hold, their heads do know,
And knowing, love, and loving, lay apart
As sacred things, far from all danger's show.
  But that rich fool, who by blind Fortune's lot
The richest gem of love and life enjoys,
And can with foul abuse such beauties blot;
Let him, deprived of sweet but unfelt joys,
  (Exil'd for aye from those high treasures, which
  He knows not) grow in only folly rich.

Rich see Introduction, p.18; *Tantal* see endnote, p.172

25

The wisest scholar[†] of the wight most wise[†]
By Phoebus' doom[†], with sug'red sentence[†] says,
That Virtue, if it once met with our eyes,
Strange flames of Love it in our souls would raise;
　　But for that man with pain this truth descries,
While he each thing in sense's balance weighs,
And so nor will, nor can, behold those skies
Which inward sun[†] to heroic mind displays,
　　Virtue of late, with virtuous care to stir
Love of herself, takes Stella's shape, that she
To mortal eyes might sweetly shine in her.
It is most true, for since I her did see,
　　Virtue's great beauty in that face I prove[†],
　　And find th'effect, for I do burn in love.

wisest scholar Plato; *wight most wise* Socrates; *Phoebus' doom* i.e. judged "most wise" by Apollo's oracle at Delphi; *sug'red sentence* see *Defence*, p.135; *inward sun* see Sonnet 71; *prove* logically/by experience

26

Though dusty[†] wits dare scorn astrology,
And fools can think those lamps of purest light,
Whose numbers, ways, greatness, eternity,
Promising wonders, wonder to invite,
　　To have for no cause birthright in the sky,
But for to spangle the black weeds of night:
Or for some brawl[†], which in that chamber high,
They should still dance to please a gazer's sight.
　　For me, I do Nature unidle know,
And know great causes, great effects procure:
And know those bodies high reign on the low.
And if these rules did fail, proof makes me sure,
　　Who oft fore-judge my after-following race,
　　By only those two stars in Stella's face.

dusty earthbound; *brawl* French dance

Because I oft in dark abstracted guise,
   Seem most alone in greatest company,
   With dearth of words, or answers quite awry,
To them that would make speech of speech arise,
They deem, and of their doom the rumour flies,
   That poison foul of bubbling pride doth lie
   So in my swelling breast that only I[†]
Fawn on myself, and others do despise:
   Yet pride I think doth not my soul possess,
Which looks too oft in his unflatt'ring glass:
But one worse fault, ambition, I confess,
That makes me oft my best friends overpass,
   Unseen, unheard, while thought to highest place
   Bends all his powers, even unto Stella's grace.

only I all I do is

You with that allegory's curious[†] frame,
   Of others' children changelings use to make,
   With me those pains for God's sake do not take:
I list not dig so deep for brazen fame.
When I say "Stella", I do mean the same
   Princess of Beauty, for whose only sake
   The reins of Love I love, though never slake[†],
And joy therein, though nations count it shame.
   I beg no subject to use[†] eloquence,
Nor in hid ways to guide philosophy:
Look at my hands for no such quintessence[†];
But know that I in pure simplicity,
   Breathe out the flames which burn within my heart,
   Love only reading unto me this art.

curious studious/inquisitive; *slake* slack; *beg...use* seek no topic merely for;
quintessence rarest fifth essence

29

Like some weak lords, neighbour'd by mighty kings,
   To keep themselves and their chief cities free,
   Do eas'ly yield, that all their coasts† may be
Ready to store their camps† of needful things:
So Stella's heart, finding what power Love brings,
   To keep itself in life and liberty,
   Doth willing grant, that in the frontiers he
Use all to help his other conquerings:
And thus her heart escapes, but thus her eyes
   Serve him with shot, her lips his heralds are:
   Her breasts his tents, legs his triumphal car:
Her flesh his food, her skin his armour brave,
And I, but for because my prospect† lies
Upon that coast, am giv'n up for a slave.

†heir coasts "weak lords"; *their camps* "mighty kings"; *prospect* gaze

30*

Whether the Turkish new-moon minded be
   To fill his horns this year on Christian coast:
   How Poles' right king means, without leave of host,
To warm with ill-made fire cold Muscovy;
If French can yet three parts in one agree;
   What now the Dutch in their full diets boast;
   How Holland hearts, now so good towns be lost,
Trust in the shade of pleasing Orange tree;
   How Ulster likes of that same golden bit,
Wherewith my father once made it half tame;
If in the Scottish Court be welt'ring yet;
These questions busy wits to me do frame;
   I, cumb'red with good manners, answer do,
   But know not how, for still I think of you.

With how sad steps, O moon, thou climb'st the skies,
  How silently, and with how wan a face,
  What may it be, that even in heav'nly place
That busy archer his sharp arrows tries?
Sure if that long with Love acquainted eyes
  Can judge of Love, thou feel'st a lover's case;
  I read it in thy looks, thy languisht grace,
To me that feel the like, thy state descries.
  Then ev'n of fellowship, O moon, tell me
Is constant love deem'd there but want of wit?
Are beauties there as proud as here they be?
Do they above love to be lov'd, and yet
  Those lovers scorn whom that Love doth possess?
  Do they call Virtue there ungratefulness*?

32

Morpheus† the lively son of deadly sleep,
  Witness of life to them that living die:
  A prophet oft, and oft an history,
A poet eke, as humours fly or creep,
Since thou in me so sure a power doest keep,
  That never I with clos'd-up sense do lie,
  But by the work my Stella I descry,
Teaching blind eyes both how to smile and weep,
  Vouchsafe of all acquaintance this to tell,
Whence hast thou ivory, rubies, pearl and gold,
To show her skin, lips, teeth and head so well?
"Fool," answers he, "no Indes such treasures hold,
  But from thy heart, while my sire charmeth thee,
  Sweet Stella's image I do steal to me."

Morpheus son of Somnus, makes humans appear in dreams

I might, unhappy word, O me, I might,
And then would not, or could not see my bliss:
Till now, wrapt in a most infernal night,
I find how heav'nly day wretch I did miss.
    Heart rent thyself, thou doest thyself but right,
No lovely Paris made thy Helen his:
No force, no fraud, robb'd thee of thy delight,
Nor Fortune of thy fortune author is:
    But to myself myself did give the blow,
While too much wit (forsooth) so troubled me,
That I respects[†] for both our sakes must show:
And yet could not by rising morn foresee
    How fair a day was near, O punisht eyes,
    That I had been more foolish or more wise.

respects caution

Come let me write, and to what end? To ease
    A burth'ned heart. How can words ease, which are
    The glasses of thy daily vexing care?
Oft cruel fights well pictured forth do please.
Art not asham'd to publish thy disease?
    Nay, that may breed my fame, it is so rare:
    But will not wise men think thy words fond ware?
Then be they close[†], and so none shall displease.
    What idler thing, than speak and not be hard?[†]
What harder thing than smart, and not to speak?
Peace, foolish wit, with wit my wit is marr'd.
Thus write I while I doubt to write, and wreak
    My harms on ink's poor loss, perhaps some find
    Stella's great pow'rs, that so confuse my mind.

they words; *close* secret; *hard* i.e. heard

35

What may words say, or what may words not say,
Where truth itself must speak like flattery?
Within what bounds can one his liking stay,
Where Nature doth with infinite agree?
   What Nestor's counsel[†] can my flames allay,
Since Reason's self doth blow the coal in me?
And ah what hope, that hope should once see day,
Where Cupid is sworn page to Chastity?
Honour is honour'd, that thou doest possess
   Him as thy slave, and now long needy Fame
   Doth even grow rich[†], naming my Stella's name.
Wit learns in thee perfection to express,
   Not thou by praise, but praise in thee is rais'd:
   It is a praise to praise, when thou art prais'd.

Nestor wise counsellor of the Greeks; *rich* see Sonnet 24

36

Stella, whence doth this new assault arise,
A conquer'd, yelden[†], ransackt heart to win?
Whereto long since, through my long batt'red eyes,
Whole armies of thy beauties ent'red in.
   And there long since, Love thy lieutenant lies,
My forces raz'd, thy banners rais'd within:
Of conquest, do not these effects suffice,
But wilt new war upon thine own begin?
   With so sweet voice, and by sweet nature so,
In sweetest strength, so sweetly skill'd withal,
In all sweet stratagems, sweet art can show,
That not my[†] soul, which at thy foot did fall,
   Long since forc'd by thy beams, but stone nor tree
   By sense's privilege, can scape from thee.

yelden yielded/wearied; *not my* not only my

37

My mouth doth water, and my breast doth swell,
  My tongue doth itch, my thoughts in labour be:
  Listen then lordings with good ear to me,
For of my life I must a riddle tell.
Towards Aurora's Court[†] a nymph doth dwell,
  Rich[†] in all beauties which man's eye can see:
  Beauties so far from reach of words that we
Abase her praise, saying she doth excel:
Rich in the treasure of deserv'd renown,
Rich in the riches of a royal heart,
Rich in those gifts which give th'eternal crown;
Who though most rich in these and every part,
  Which make the patents[†] of true worldly bliss,
  Hath no misfortune, but that Rich she is.

Aurora's Court in the east (Aurora, goddess of the dawn); *Rich* see Sonnets 24, 35; *patents* titles of possession

38

This night while sleep begins with heavy wings
  To hatch[†] mine eyes, and that unbitted[†] thought
  Doth fall to stray, and my chief powers are brought
To leave[†] the sceptre of all subject things,
The first that straight my fancy's error[†] brings
  Unto my mind, is Stella's image, wrought
  By Love's own self, but with so curious draught[†],
That she, methinks, not only shines but sings.
  I start, look, hark, but what in clos'd up sense
Was held, in open'd sense it flies away,
Leaving me nought but wailing eloquence:
I seeing better sights in sight's decay,
  Call'd it anew, and wooed sleep again:
  But him her host that unkind guest had slain.

hatch close; *unbitted* unbridled; *leave* surrender; *error* wandering; *draught* drawing

Come sleep, O sleep, the certain knot of peace,
The baiting† place of wit, the balm of woe,
The poor man's wealth, the prisoner's release,
Th'indifferent judge between the high and low;
   With shield of proof† shield me from out the prease†
Of those fierce darts, despair at me doth throw:
O make me in those civil wars to cease;
I will good tribute pay if thou do so.
   Take thou of me smooth pillows, sweetest bed,
A chamber deaf to noise, and blind to light:
A rosy garland†, and a weary head:
And if these things, as being thine by right,
   Move not thy heavy grace, thou shalt in me,
   Livelier than elsewhere Stella's image see.

baiting resting; *of proof* tested; *prease* throng; *rosy garland* rose as an emblem of silence

As good to write as for to lie and groan,
   O Stella dear, how much thy power hath wrought,
   That hast my mind, none of the basest, brought
My still kept course, while others sleep, to moan.
Alas, if from the height of Virtue's throne,
   Thou canst vouchsafe the influence of a thought
   Upon a wretch, that long thy grace hath sought;
Weigh then how I by thee am overthrown:
   And then, think thus, although thy beauty be
   Made manifest by such a victory,
Yet noblest conquerors do wrecks avoid.
   Since then thou hast so far subdued me,
   That in my heart I offer still to thee,
O do not let thy temple be destroy'd.

Having this day my horse, my hand, my lance
  Guided so well, that I obtain'd the prize,
  Both by the judgement of the English eyes,
And of some sent from that sweet enemy France;
Horsemen my skill in horsemanship advance[†],
  Town-folks my strength; a daintier[†] judge applies
  His praise to sleight[†], which from good use[†] doth rise;
Some lucky wits impute it but to chance;
  Others, because of both sides[†] I do take
My blood from them, who did excel in this,
Think Nature me a man of arms did make.
How far they shoot awry! the true cause is,
  Stella look'd on, and from her heavenly face
  Sent forth the beams, which made so fair my race.

advance praise; *daintier* more demanding; *sleight* dexterity; *good use* practice; *both sides* i.e. on both sides of his family

O eyes, which do the spheres of beauty move,
Whose beams be joys, whose joys all virtues be,
Who while they make Love conquer, conquer Love,
The schools where Venus hath learn'd chastity.
  O eyes, where humble looks most glorious prove,
Only lov'd tyrants, just in cruelty,
Do not, O do not from poor me remove,
Keep still my zenith, ever shine on me.
  For though I never see them, but straightways
My life forgets to nourish languisht sprites;
Yet still on me, O eyes, dart down your rays:
And if from majesty of sacred lights,
  Oppressing mortal sense, my death proceed,
  Wracks triumphs be, which Love (high set) doth breed.

Fair eyes, sweet lips, dear heart, that foolish I
Could hope by Cupid's help on you to prey;
Since to himself he doth your gifts apply,
As his main force, choice sport, and easeful stay.
    For when he will see who dare him gainsay,
Then with those eyes he looks, lo by and by[†]
Each soul doth at Love's feet his weapons lay,
Glad if for her he give them leave to die.
    When he will play, then in her lips he is,
Where blushing red, that Love's self them doth love,
With either lip he doth the other kiss:
But when he will for quiet's sake remove
    From all the world, her heart is then his rome[†],
    Where well he knows, no man to him can come.

by and by immediately; *rome* old spelling of both "room" and "roam"

My words I know do well set forth my mind,
    My mind bemoans his sense of inward smart;
    Such smart may pity claim of any heart,
Her heart, sweet heart, is of no tiger's kind:
And yet she hears, yet I no pity find;
    But more I cry, less grace she doth impart,
    Alas, what cause is there so overthwart[†],
That nobleness itself makes thus unkind?[†]
    I much do guess, yet find no truth save this,
That when the breath of my complaints doth touch
Those dainty doors unto the Court of bliss,
The heav'nly nature of that place is such,
    That once come there, the sobs of mine annoys
    Are metamorphos'd straight to tunes of joys.

overthwart in opposition; *unkind* also, unnatural

45

Stella oft sees the very face of woe
　　Painted in my beclouded stormy face:
　　But cannot skill[†] to pity my disgrace,
Not though thereof the cause herself she know:
Yet hearing late a fable, which did show
　　Of lovers never known, a grievous case,
　　Pity thereof gat in her breast such place,
That from that sea deriv'd, tears' spring did flow.
　　Alas, if Fancy drawn by imag'd things,
Though false, yet with free scope more grace doth breed
Than servant's wrack, where new doubts* honour brings;
Then think my dear, that you in me do read
　　Of lover's ruin some sad tragedy:
　　I am not I, pity the tale of me.

cannot skill does not know how

46

I curst thee oft, I pity now thy case,
　　Blind-hitting boy, since she that thee and me
　　Rules with a beck, so tyrannizeth thee,
That thou must want or food, or dwelling place.
For she protests to banish thee her face,
　　Her face? O Love, a rogue[†] thou then shouldst be!
　　If Love learn not alone[†] to love and see,
Without desire to feed of further grace.
　　Alas poor wag, that now a scholar art
To such a school-mistress, whose lessons new
Thou needs must miss[†], and so thou needs must smart.
Yet dear, let me this pardon get of you,
　　So long (though he from book myche[†] to desire)
　　Till without fuel you can make hot fire.

rogue nameless vagrant; *if...not alone* unless Love learns only; *needs...miss*
neglect/fail to understand; *myche* play truant

What, have I thus betrayed my liberty?
  Can those black beams† such burning marks† engrave
  In my free side? or am I born a slave,
Whose neck becomes† such yoke of tyranny?
Or want I sense to feel my misery?
  Or sprite, disdain of such disdain to have?
  Who for long faith, tho' daily help I crave,
May get no alms but scorn of beggary.
  Virtue awake, Beauty but beauty is,
I may, I must, I can, I will, I do
Leave following that, which it is gain to miss.
Let her go. Soft, but here she comes. Go to,
  Unkind, I love you not: O me, that eye
  Doth make my heart give to my tongue the lie.

lack beams Stella's glance; *burning marks* brands of slavery; *becomes* suits

Soul's joy, bend not those morning stars from me,
  Where Virtue is made strong by Beauty's might,
  Where Love is chasteness, Pain doth learn delight,
And Humbleness grows one with Majesty.
Whatever may ensue, O let me be
  Copartner of the riches of that sight:
  Let not mine eyes be hell-driv'n from that light:
O look, O shine, O let me die and see.
  For though I oft myself of them bemoan,
  That through my heart their beamy darts be gone,
Whose cureless wounds even now most freshly bleed:
  Yet since my death-wound is already got.
  Dear killer, spare not thy sweet cruel shot:
A kind of grace it is to slay with speed.

I on my horse, and Love on me doth try
    Our horsemanships, while by strange work I prove
    A horseman to my horse, a horse to Love;
And now man's wrongs in me, poor beast, descry.
The reins wherewith my rider doth me tie,
    Are humbled thoughts, which bit of reverence move,
    Curb'd in with fear, but with guilt boss† above
Of Hope, which makes it seem fair to the eye.
    The wand† is Will, thou Fancy saddle art,
Girt fast by memory, and while I spur
My horse, he spurs with sharp desire my heart:
He sits me fast, however I do stir:
    And now hath made me to his hand so right,
    That in the manage† myself takes delight.

guilt play on "gilt"; *boss* metal stud; *wand* riding crop; *manage* being trained/handled

Stella, the fulness of my thoughts of thee
Cannot be stay'd within my panting breast,
But they do swell and struggle forth of me,
Till that in words thy figure be exprest.
    And yet as soon as they so formed be,
According to my lord Love's own behest:
With sad† eyes I their weak proportion see,
To portrait that which in this world is best.
    So that I cannot choose but write my mind,
And cannot choose but put out† what I write,
While those poor babes their death in birth do find:
And now my pen these lines had dashed quite,
    But that they stopt his fury from the same,
    Because their forefront bare sweet Stella's name.

sad also, serious; *put out* strike out

Pardon mine ears, both I and they do pray,
  So may your tongue still fluently proceed,
  To them that do such entertainment need,
So may you still have somewhat new to say.
On silly[†] me do not the burthen lay,
  Of all the grave conceits your brain doth breed;
  But find some Hercules[†] to bear, instead
Of Atlas tir'd, your wisdom's heav'nly sway[†].
  For me, while you discourse of courtly tides,
Of cunning fishers in most troubled streams,
Of straying ways, when valiant error guides:
Meanwhile my heart confers with Stella's beams,
  And is even irkt that so sweet comedy,
  By such unsuited speech should hind'red be.

silly simple; *Hercules* Hercules temporarily relieved Atlas of his burden of the heavens; *sway* pressure

A strife[†] is grown between Virtue and Love,
  While each pretends[†] that Stella must be his:
  Her eyes, her lips, her all, saith Love do this,
Since they do wear his badge[†], most firmly prove.
But Virtue thus that title doth disprove,
  That Stella (O dear name) that Stella is
  That virtuous soul, sure heir of heav'nly bliss:
Not this fair outside, which our hearts doth move.
  And therefore, though her beauty and her grace
Be Love's indeed, in Stella's self he may
By no pretence claim any manner place.
Well Love, since this demur[†] our suit[†] doth stay,
  Let Virtue have that Stella's self; yet thus,
  That Virtue but that body grant to us.

A strife see Introduction, p.20; *pretends* legally claims; *badge* livery; *demur* legal plea; *suit* of lover or lawyer

In martial sports I had my cunning tried,
   And yet to brake more staves did me address:
   While with the people's shouts I must confess,
Youth, luck, and praise, even fill'd my veins with pride.
When Cupid, having me his slave descried
   In Mars's livery, prancing in the press[†]:
   "What now sir fool," said he, "I would no less,
Look here, I say." I look'd, and Stella spied,
   Who hard by made a window send forth light;
My heart then quak'd, then dazzled were mine eyes,
One hand forgot to rule, th'other to fight.
Nor trumpets' sound I heard, nor friendly cries;
   My foe came on, and beat the air for me,
   Till that her blush taught me my shame to see.

press throng

Because I breathe not love to every one,
   Nor do not use set colours for to wear,
   Nor nourish special locks of vowed hair,
Nor give each speech a full point[†] of a groan,
The courtly nymphs, acquainted with the moan
   Of them, who in their lips Love's standard bear;
   "What he?" say they of me, "now I dare swear,
He cannot love: no, no, let him alone."
   And[†] think so still, so Stella know my mind,
Profess in deed I do not Cupid's art;
But you fair maids, at length this true shall find,
That his right badge is but worn in the heart:
   Dumb swans, no chatt'ring pies[†], do lovers prove,
   They love indeed, who quake to say they love.

full point full stop; *And* i.e. let them; *pies* magpies

Muses, I oft invoke your holy aid,
    With choicest flowers[†] my speech to engarland so;
    That it, despis'd in true in true but naked show,
Might win some grace in your sweet grace array'd[†],
And oft whole troops[†] of saddest words I stay'd,
    Striving·abroad a-foraging to go;
    Until by your inspiring I might know,
How their black banner might be best display'd.
    But now I mean no more your help to try,
Nor other sug'ring of my speech to prove,
But on her name incessantly to cry:
For let me but name her whom I do love,
    So sweet sounds straight mine ear and heart do hit,
    That I well find no eloquence like it.

flowers see Sonnet 15; *array'd* dressed/ordered like troops; *troops* with pun on "tropes"

Fie, school of Patience, fie, your lesson is
    Far far too long to learn it without book[†]:
    What, a whole week without one piece of look,
And think I should not your large precepts miss?[†]
When I might read those letters fair of bliss,
    Which in her face teach virtue, I could brook
    Somewhat thy lead'n counsels, which I took,
As of a friend that meant not much amiss:
    But now that I, alas, do want[†] her sight,
What, dost thou think that I can ever take
In thy cold stuff a phlegmatic[†] delight?
No Patience, if thou wilt my good, then make
    Her come, and hear with patience my desire,
    And then with patience bid me bear my fire.

without book by memory; *miss* forget; *want* lack; *phlegmatic* the cold, moist humour

Woe, having made with many fights his own
  Each sense of mine, each gift, each power of mind,
  Grown now his slaves, he forc'd them out to find
The thorowest[†] words, fit for woe's self to groan,
Hoping that when they might find Stella alone,
  Before she could prepare to be unkind,
  Her soul arm'd but with such a dainty rind,
Should soon be pierc'd with sharpness of the moan.
  She heard my plaints, and did not only hear,
But them (so sweet is she) most sweetly sing,
With that fair breast making woe's darkness clear: ʼ
A pretty case – I hoped her to bring
  To feel my griefs, and she with face and voice
  So sweets my pains, that my pains me rejoice.

thorowest penetrating

58

Doubt there hath been when with his golden chain[†],
  The orator so far men's hearts doth bind,
  That no pace else their guided steps can find,
But as he them more short or slack doth rein,
Whether with words this sovereignty he gain,
  Cloth'd with fine tropes, with strongest reasons lin'd[†],
  Or else pronouncing grace[†], wherewith his mind
Prints his own lively form in rudest brain:
  Now judge by this, in piercing phrases late,
  Th'anatomy of all my woes I wrate,
Stella's sweet breath the same to me did read.
  O voice, O face, maugre[†] my speech's might,
  Which wooed woe, most ravishing delight,
Even those sad words even in sad me did breed.

golden chain emblem of eloquence; *tropes, reasons* see Sonnet 3; *pronouncing grace*
delivery; *maugre* despite

Dear, why make you more of a dog than me?
    If he do love, I burn, I burn in love:
    If he wait well, I never thence would move:
If he be fair, yet but a dog can be.
Little he is, so little worth is he;
    He barks, my songs thine own voice oft doth prove[†]:
    Bidd'n, perhaps he fetcheth thee a glove,
But I unbid, fetch even my soul to thee.
    Yet while I languish, him that bosom clips[†],
That lap doth lap, nay lets in spite of spite,
This sour-breath'd mate taste of those sug'red lips.
Alas, if you grant only such delight
    To witless things, then Love, I hope (since wit
    Becomes a clog[†]) will soon ease me of it.

prove try; *clips* embraces; *clog* wooden encumbrance

When my good angel guides me to the place,
    Where all my good I do in Stella see,
    That heav'n of joys throws only down on me
Thund'red disdains and lightnings of disgrace:
But when the rugged'st step of Fortune's race
    Makes me fall from her sight, then sweetly she
    With words, wherein the Muses' treasures be,
Shows love and pity to my absent case.
    Now I wit-beaten long by hardest Fate,
So dull am, that I cannot look into
The ground of this fierce love and lovely hate:
Then some good body tell me how I do,
    Whose presence, absence, absence presence is;
    Blist in my curse, and cursed in my bliss.

61

Oft with true sighs, oft with uncalled tears,
Now with slow words, now with dumb eloquence
I Stella's eyes assail, invade her ears;
But this at last is her sweet breath'd defence:
    That who indeed infelt affection bears,
So captives to his saint both soul and sense,
That wholly hers, all selfness he forbears,
Thence his desires he learns, his love's course thence.
    Now since her chaste mind hates this love in me,
    With chast'ned mind, I straight must show that she
Shall quickly me from what she hates remove.
    O Doctor† Cupid, thou for me reply,
    Driv'n else to grant by angel's sophistry,
That I love not, without I leave to† love.

Doctor of Philosophy; *leave to* stop

62

Late tir'd with woe, even ready for to pine
With rage of Love, I call'd my love unkind;
She in whose eyes Love though unfelt doth shine,
Sweet said that I true love in her should find.
    I joyed, but straight thus wat'red was my wine,
That love she did, but loved a Love not blind,
Which would not let me, whom she loved, decline
From nobler course, fit for my birth and mind:
    And therefore by her Love's authority,
    Will'd me these tempests of vain love to fly,
And anchor fast myself on Virtue's shore.
    Alas, if this the only metal be
    Of Love, new-coin'd to help my beggary,
Dear, love me not, that you may love me more.

O grammar rules, O now your virtues show;
  So children still read you with awful[†] eyes,
  As my young dove may in your precepts wise
Her grant to me, by her own virtue know.
For late with heart most high, with eyes most low,
  I crav'd the thing which ever she denies:
  She light'ning Love, displaying Venus' skies,
Least once should not be heard, twice said, No, No.
  Sing then my Muse, now *Io Pean*[†] sing,
  Heav'ns envy not at my high triumphing:
But grammar's force with sweet success[†] confirm:
  For grammar says (O this dear Stella weigh,)
  For grammar says (to grammar who says nay)
That in one speech two negatives affirm.

awful respectful; *Io Pean* hymn of praise; *success* also, result

First song

Doubt you to whom my Muse these notes intendeth,
Which now my breast orecharg'd to music lendeth:
To you, to you, all song of praise is due,
Only in you my song begins and endeth.

Who hath the eyes which marry state with pleasure,
Who keeps the key of Nature's chiefest treasure:
To you, to you, all song of praise is due,
Only for you the heav'n forgat all measure.

Who hath the lips, where wit in fairness reigneth,
Who womankind at once both decks and staineth[†]:
To you, to you, all song of praise is due,
Only by you Cupid his crown maintaineth.

staineth deprives of lustre

Who hath the feet, whose step all sweetness planteth
Who else for whom Fame worthy trumpets wanteth:
To you, to you, all song of praise is due,
Only to you her sceptre Venus granteth.

Who hath the breast, whose milk doth passions nourish,
Whose grace is such, that when it chides doth cherish:
To you, to you, all song of praise is due,
Only through you the tree of life doth flourish.

Who hath the hand which without stroke subdueth,
Who long dead beauty with increase reneweth:
To you, to you, all song of praise is due,
Only at you all envy hopeless rueth.

Who hath the hair which loosest fastest tieth,
Who makes a man live then glad when he dieth:
To you, to you, all song of praise is due:
Only of you the flatterer never lieth.

Who hath the voice, which soul from senses sunders,
Whose force but yours the bolts of beauty thunders:
To you, to you, all song of praise is due:
Only with you not miracles are wonders.

Doubt you to whom my Muse these notes intendeth,
Which now my breast orecharg'd to music lendeth:
To you, to you, all song of praise is due:
Only in you my song begins and endeth.

64

No more, my dear, no more these counsels try,
  O give my passions leave to run their race:
  Let Fortune lay on me her worst disgrace,
Let folk orecharg'd with brain against me cry.
Let clouds bedim my face, break in mine eye,
  Let me no steps but of lost labour trace,
  Let all the earth with scorn recount my case,
But do not will me from my love to fly.
  I do not envy Aristotle's wit,
Nor do aspire to Caesar's bleeding fame,
Nor aught do care, though some above me sit,
Nor hope, nor wish another course to frame,
  But that which once may win thy cruel heart,
  Thou art my wit, and thou my virtue art.

65

Love by sure proof I may call thee unkind,
That giv'st no better ear to my just cries:
Thou whom to me such my good turns should bind,
As I may well recount, but none can prize[†]:
  For when nak'd boy thou couldst no harbour find
In this old world, grown now so too too wise:
I lodg'd thee in my heart, and being blind
By Nature born, I gave to thee mine eyes.
  Mine eyes, my light, my heart, my life, alas,
If so great services may scorned be:
Yet let this thought thy tigrish courage pass[†]:
That I perhaps am somewhat kin to thee;
  Since in thine arms[†], if learn'd fame truth hath spread,
  Thou bear'st the arrow, I the arrow head.

prize evaluate; *pass* pierce; *arms* play on heraldry; Sidney's own device included an arrow-head

66

And do I see some cause a hope to feed,
   Or doth the tedious burd'n of long woe
   In weakened minds, quick apprehending breed,
Of every image, which may comfort show?
   I cannot brag of word, much less of deed,
   Fortune wheels still with me in one sort slow[†],
   My wealth no more, and no whit less my need,
Desire still on the stilts[†] of fear doth go.
   And yet amid all fears a hope there is
   Stol'n to my heart since last fair night, nay day[†],
   Stella's eyes sent to me the beams of bliss,
Looking on me, while I lookt other way:
      But when mine eyes back to their heav'n did move,
      They fled with blush, which guilty seem'd of love.

in...slow with unvarying slowness; *stilts* crutches; *night...day* Stella's eyes turn to day

67

Hope, art thou true, or dost thou flatter me?
   Doth Stella now begin with piteous eye,
   The ruins of her conquest to espie:
Will she take time[†], before all wracked be?
Her eye's-speech is translated thus by thee:
   But fail'st thou not in phrase so heav'nly high?
   Look on again, the fair text better try:
What blushing notes doest thou in margin see?
   What sighs stol'n out, or kill'd before full born?
Hast thou found such and such like arguments?[†]
Or art thou else to comfort me foresworn?[†]
Well, how so thou interpret the contents,
   I am resolv'd thy error to maintain,
   Rather than by more truth to get more pain.

take time relent; *arguments* evidence; *foresworn* falsely sworn

Stella, the only planet of my light,
  Light of my life, and life of my desire,
  Chief good, whereto my hope doth only aspire,
World of my wealth, and heav'n of my delight.
Why doest thou spend the treasures of thy sprite,
  With voice more fit to wed Amphion's lyre[†],
  Seeking to quench in me the noble fire,
Fed by thy worth, and kindled by thy sight?
  And all in vain, for while thy breath most sweet,
  With choicest words, thy words with reasons rare,
Thy reasons firmly set on Virtue's feet,
Labour to kill in me this killing care:
  O think I then, what paradise of joy
  It is, so fair a Virtue to enjoy.

Amphion see note, p.170

O joy, too high for my low style to show:
  O bliss, fit for a nobler state than me:
  Envy, put out thine eyes, lest thou do see
What oceans of delight in me do flow.
My friend, that oft saw through all masks my woe,
  Come, come, and let me pour myself on thee;
  Gone is the winter of my misery,
My spring appears, O see what here doth grow.
  For Stella hath with words where faith doth shine,
Of her high heart given me the monarchy:
I, I, O I may say, that she is mine.
And though she give but thus condition'ly
  This realm of bliss, while virtuous course I take,
  No kings be crown'd, but they some covenants make.

70

My Muse may well grudge at my heav'nly joy,
If I still force her in sad rhymes to creep:
She oft hath drunk my tears, now hopes to enjoy
Nectar of mirth, since I Jove's cup do keep†.
   Sonnets† be not bound prentice to annoy:
Trebles sing high, as well as basses deep:
Grief but Love's winter livery is, the boy
Hath cheeks to smile, as well as eyes to weep.
   Come then my Muse, show thou height of delight
In well rais'd notes, my pen the best it may
Shall paint out joy, though but in black and white.
Cease eager Muse, peace pen, for my sake stay,
   I give you here my hand for truth of this,
   Wise silence is best music unto bliss.

Jove's…keep like Ganymede, see sonnet 13; *sonnets* includes sense of song/melody

71

Who will in fairest book of Nature know,
   How Virtue may best lodg'd in beauty be,
   Let him but learn of Love to read in thee
Stella, those fair lines, which true goodness show.
There shall he find all vices' overthrow,
   Not by rude force, but sweetest sovereignty
   Of reason, from whose light those night-birds fly;
That inward sun in thine eyes shineth so.
   And not content to be perfection's heir
Thyself, doest strive all minds that way to move:
Who mark in thee what is in thee most fair.
So while thy beauty draws the heart to love,
   As fast thy Virtue bends that love to good:
   "But ah," Desire still cries, "give me some food."

Desire, though thou my old companion art,
   And oft so clings to my pure love, that I
   One from the other scarcely can descry,
While each doth blow the fire of my heart;
Now from thy fellowship I needs must part,
   Venus is taught with Dian's wings to fly:
   I must no more in thy sweet passions lie;
Virtue's gold now must head my Cupid's dart.
   Service and honour, wonder with delight,
Fear to offend, will worthy to appear,
Care shining in mine eyes, faith in my sprite.
These things are left me by my only dear;
   But thou Desire, because thou wouldst have all,
   Now banisht art, but yet alas how shall?

Second song

Have I caught my heav'nly jewel,
Teaching sleep most fair to be?
Now will I teach her that she,
When she wakes, is too cruel.

Since sweet sleep her eyes hath charmed,
The two only darts of Love:
Now will I with that boy prove
Some play, while he is disarmed.

Her tongue waking still refuseth,
Giving frankly niggard No:
Now will I attempt to know,
What No her tongue sleeping useth.

See the hand which waking guardeth,
Sleeping, grants a free resort:
Now will I invade the fort;
Cowards Love with loss rewardeth.

But O fool, think of the danger,
Of her just and high disdain:
Now will I alas refrain,
Love fears nothing else but anger.

Yet those lips so sweetly smelling,
Do invite a stealing kiss:
Now will I but venture this,
Who will read must first learn spelling.

Oh sweet kiss, but ah she is waking,
Low'ring beauty chastens me:
Now will I away hence flee:
Fool, more fool, for no more taking.

73

Love still a boy, and oft a wanton is,
School'd only by his mother's tender eye:
What wonder then if he his lesson miss†,
When for so soft a rod dear play he try?
   And yet my star, because a sug'red kiss
In sport I suckt, while she asleep did lie,
Doth lower, nay, chide; nay, threat for only this:
Sweet, it was saucy Love, not humble I.
   But no 'scuse serves, she makes her wrath appear
   In Beauty's throne, see now who dares come near
Those scarlet judges, threat'ning bloody pain?
   O heav'nly fool, thy most kiss-worthy face,
   Anger invests with such a lovely grace,
That Anger's self I needs must kiss again.

miss neglect/fail to understand

I never drank of Aganippe well,
Nor ever did in shade of Tempe sit:[†]
And Muses scorn with vulgar brains to dwell,
Poor layman I, for sacred rites unfit.
   Some do I hear of poets' fury[†] tell,
But (God wot) wot not what they mean by it:
And this I swear by blackest brook of hell,
I am no pick-purse of another's wit.
   How falls it then, that with so smooth an ease
My thoughts I speak, and what I speak doth flow
In verse, and that my verse best wits doth please?
Guess we the cause: "What, is it thus?" Fie no:
   "Or so?" Much less: "How then?" Sure thus it is:
   My lips are sweet, inspired with Stella's kiss.

Aganippe, Tempe places sacred to poetry; *fury* inspiration

*Of all the kings that ever here did reign
Edward named fourth, as first in praise I name,
Not for his fair outside, nor well lined brain,
Although less gifts imp feathers oft on Fame
   Nor that he could young-wise, wise-valiant frame
His sire's revenge, join'd with a kingdom's gain:
And gain'd by Mars, could yet mad Mars so tame,
That balance weigh'd what sword did late obtain.
   Nor that he made the Flouredeluce so 'fraid,
Though strongly hedg'd[†] of bloody lion's paws,
That witty Lewis to him a tribute paid.
Nor this, nor that, nor any such small cause,
   But only for this worthy knight durst prove
   To lose his crown, rather than fail his love.

hedg'd bordered

76

She comes, and straight therewith her shining twins do move
   Their rays to me, who in her tedious absence lay
   Benighted in cold woe, but now appears my day,
The only light of joy, the only warmth of love.
She comes with light and warmth, which like Aurora prove
   Of gentle force, so that mine eyes dare gladly play
   With such a rosy morn, whose beams most freshly gay
Scorch not, but only do dark chilling sprites remove.
   But lo, while I do speak, it groweth noon with me,
Her flamy glist'ring lights increase with time and place;
Her heart cries "ah", it burns, mine eyes now dazzled be:
No wind, no shade can cool, what help then in my case,
   But with short breath, long looks, stay'd feet and walking[†] head,
   Pray that my sun go down with meeker beams to bed.

walking agitated

77

Those looks, whose beams be joy, whose motion is delight,
That face, whose lecture[†] shows what perfect beauty is:
That presence, which doth give dark hearts a living light:
That grace, which Venus weeps that she herself doth miss:
   That hand, which without touch holds more than Atlas might;
Those lips, which make death's pay a mean price for a kiss:
That skin, whose pass-praise hue scorns this poor term of white:
Those words, which do sublime the quintessence[†] of bliss:
   That voice, which makes the soul plant himself in the ears:
That conversation sweet, where such high comforts be,
As constru'd in high speech, the name of heav'n it bears,
Makes me in my best thoughts and quietest judgement see,
   That in no more but these I might be fully blest:
   Yet ah, my maid'n Muse doth blush to tell the best.

whose lecture the reading of which; *sublime the quintessence* from alchemy, extract
the pure essence

78

O how the pleasant airs of true love be
    Infected by those vapours, which arise
    From out that noisome gulf, which gaping lies
Between the jaws of hellish Jealousy.
A monster, other's harm, self-misery,
    Beauty's plague, Virtue's scourge, succour of lies:
    Who his own joy to his own hurt applies,
And only cherish doth with injury.
    Who since he hath, by Nature's special grace,
    So piercing paws, as spoil when they embrace,
So nimble feet as stir still, though on thorns:
    So many eyes aye seeking their own woe,
    So ample ears as never good news know:
Is it not evil that such a devil wants horns?†

wants lacks the *horns* of the cuckold

79

Sweet kiss, thy sweets I fain would sweetly indite,
    Which even of sweetness sweetest sweet'ner art:
    Pleasingst consort†, where each sense holds a part,
Which coupling doves† guides Venus' chariot right.
Best charge, and bravest retrait† in Cupid's fight,
    A double key, which opens to the heart,
    Most rich, when most his riches it impart:
Nest of young joys, schoolmaster of delight,
    Teaching the mean, at once to take and give
The friendly fray, where blows both wound and heal,
The pretty death, while each in other live.
Poor hope's first wealth, hostage of promist weal,
    Breakfast of love, but lo, lo, where she is,
    Cease we to praise, now pray we for a kiss.

consort combination of instruments; *coupling doves* traditional drawers of Venus'
chariot; *retrait* retreat

Sweet swelling lip, well may'st thou swell in pride,
   Since best wits think it wit thee to admire;
   Nature's praise, Virtue's stall[+], Cupid's cold fire,
Whence words, not words, but heav'nly graces slide.
The new Parnassus, where the Muses bide,
   Sweetner of music, wisdom's beautifier:
   Breather of life, and fast'ner of desire,
Where Beauty's blush in Honour's grain* is dyed.
   Thus much my heart compell'd my mouth to say,
   But now spite of my heart my mouth will stay,
Loathing all lies, doubting[+] this flattery is:
   And no spur can his resty[+] race renew,
   Without[+] how far this praise is short of you,
Sweet lip, you teach my mouth with one sweet kiss.

stall seat of dignity; *doubting* fearing; *resty* restive; *without* unless

O kiss, which doest those ruddy gems impart,
Or gems[+], or fruits of new-found Paradise,
Breathing all bliss and sweet'ning to the heart,
Teaching dumb lips a nobler exercise.
   O kiss, which souls, even souls together ties
By links of Love, and only Nature's art:
How fain would I paint thee to all men's eyes,
Or of thy gifts at least shade out[+] some part.
   But she forbids, with blushing words, she says,
   She builds her fame on higher seated praise:
But my heart burns, I cannot silent be.
   Then since (dear life) you fain would have me peace,
   And I, mad with delight, want wit to cease,
Stop you my mouth with still still[+] kissing me.

gems also buds; *shade out* sketch faintly; *still still* punning on still = silent

82

Nymph of the gard'n, where all beauties be:
   Beauties which do in excellency pass
   His[†] who till death lookt in a wat'ry glass,
Or hers[†] whom naked the Trojan boy did see.
Sweet gard'n nymph, which keeps the cherry tree,
   Whose fruit doth far th'Esperian taste[†] surpass:
   Most sweet-fair, most fair-sweet, do not alas,
From coming near those cherries banish me:
   For though full of desire, empty of wit,
Admitted late by your best-graced grace,
I caught at one of them a hungry bit;
Pardon that fault, once more grant me the place,
   And I do swear even by the same delight,
   I will but kiss, I never more will bite.

His Narcissus; *hers* Venus; *th'Esperian taste* apples of the Hesperides

83

Good brother Philip[†], I have borne you long,
   I was content you should in favour creep,
   While craftily you seem'd your cut to keep[†],
As though that fair soft hand did you great wrong.
I bare (with envy) yet I bare your song,
   When in her neck you did love ditties peep;
   Nay, more fool I, oft suffered you to sleep
In lilies' nest, where Love's self lies along.
   What, doth high place ambitious thoughts augment?
Is sauciness reward of courtesy?
Cannot such grace your silly self content,
But you must needs with those lips billing be?
   And through those lips drink nectar from that tongue;
   Leave that sir Philip, lest off your neck be wrung.

Philip traditional poetic name of pet sparrow; *cut to keep* keep your distance

Third song

If Orpheus' voice had force to breathe such music's love
Through pores of senseless trees, as it could make them move:
If stones good measure danc'd, the Theban walls to build,
To cadence of the tunes, which Amphyon's lyre did yield,
More cause a like effect at leastwise bringeth:
O stones, O trees, learn hearing, Stella singeth.

If love might sweet'n so a boy of shepherd brood,*
To make a lizard dull to taste love's dainty food:
If eagle fierce could so in Grecian maid delight,*
As his light was her eyes, her death his endless night:
Earth gave that love, heav'n I trow love refineth:
O birds, O beasts, look love, lo, Stella shineth.

The birds, beasts, stones and trees feel this, and feeling love:
And if the trees, nor stones stir not the same to prove,
Nor beasts, nor birds do come unto this blessed gaze,
Know, that small love is quick, and great love doth amaze:
They are amaz'd, but you with reason armed,
O eyes, O ears of men, how are you charmed!

84

Highway since you my chief Parnassus be†,
   And that my Muse to some ears not unsweet
   Tempers her words to trampling horses' feet,
More oft than to a chamber melody;
Now blessed you, bear onward blessed me
   To her, where I my heart safeliest† shall meet,
   My Muse and I must you of duty greet
With thanks and wishes, wishing thankfully.
   Be you still fair, honour'd by public heed,
By no encroachment wrong'd, nor time forgot:
Nor blam'd for blood†, nor sham'd for sinful deed.
And that you know, I envy you no lot†

Of highest wish, I wish you so much bliss,
Hundreds of years you Stella's feet may kiss.

Highway . . . Parnassus a journey is his poetic inspiration; *safeliest* in most secret/
security; *blood* violence; *lot* fortune

85

I see the house, my heart thyself contain,
 Beware full sails drown not thy tott'ring barge:
 Lest joy, by Nature apt sprites to enlarge,
Thee to thy wrack beyond thy limits strain.
Nor do like lords, whose weak confused brain,
 Not pointing to fit folks each undercharge,
 While every office themselves will discharge,
With doing all, leave nothing done but pain.
 But give apt servants their due place, let eyes
See Beauty's total sum summ'd in her face:
Let ears hear speech, which wit to wonder ties,
Let breath suck up those sweets, let arms embrace
 The globe of weal, lips Love's indentures[†] make:
 Thou but of all the kingly tribute take.

indentures indentations/contracts

Fourth song

Only joy, now here you are,
Fit to hear and ease my care:
Let my whispering voice obtain,
Sweet reward for sharpest pain:
Take me to thee, and thee to me.
"No, no, no, no, my dear, let be."[†]

Night hath clos'd all in her cloak,
Twinkling stars love-thoughts provoke:
Danger hence good care doth keep,
Jealousy itself doth sleep:
Take me to thee, and thee to me.
"No, no, no, no, my dear, let be."

Better place no wit can find,
Cupid's yoke to loose or bind:
These sweet flowers on fine bed too,
Us in their best language woo:
Take me to thee, and thee to me.
"No, no, no, no, my dear, let be."

This small light the moon bestows,
Serves thy beams but to disclose,
So to raise my hap more high;
Fear not else, none can us spy:
Take me to thee, and thee to me.
"No, no, no, no, my dear, let be."

That you heard was but a mouse,
Dumb sleep holdeth all the house:
Yet asleep, methinks they say,
Young folks, take time while you may:
Take me to thee, and thee to me.
"No, no, no, no, my dear, let be."

Niggard Time threats, if we miss
This large offer of our bliss,
Long stay ere he grant the same:
Sweet then, while each thing doth frame:
Take me to thee, and thee to me.
"No, no, no, no, my dear, let be."

Your fair mother is abed,
Candles out and curtains spread:
She thinks you do letters write,
Write, but first let me indite:
Take me to thee, and thee to me.
"No, no, no, no, my dear, let be."

Sweet alas, why strive you thus?
Concord better fitteth us:
Leave to Mars the force of hands,
Your power in your beauty stands:
Take me to thee, and thee to me.
"No, no, no, no, my dear, let be."

Woe to me, and do you swear
Me to hate? But I forbear,
Cursed be my destines all,
That brought me so high to fall:
Take me to thee, and thee to me.
"No, no, no, no, my dear, let be."

No, no the last line of each stanza is Stella's reply

86

Alas, whence came this change of looks? If I
   Have chang'd desert, let mine own conscience be
   A still felt plague, to self condemning me:
Let woe gripe on my heart, shame load mine eye.
But if all faith, like spotless ermine lie
   Safe in my soul, which only doth to thee
   (As his sole object of felicity)
With wings of Love in air of wonder fly,
   O ease your hand, treat not so hard your slave:
In justice pains come not till faults do call;
Or if I needs (sweet judge) must torments have,
Use something else to chast'n me withall
   Than those blest eyes, where all my hopes do dwell,
   No doom should make one's heav'n become his hell.

Fifth song

While favour fed my hope, and delight with hope was brought,
Thought waited on delight, and speech did follow thought:
Then grew my tongue and pen records unto thy glory:
I thought all words were lost, that were not spent of thee:
I thought each place was dark but where thy lights would be,
And all ears worse than deaf, that heard not out thy story.

I said, thou wert most fair, and so indeed thou art:
I said, thou wert most sweet, sweet poison to my heart:
I said, my soul was thine (O that I then had lied)
I said, thine eyes were stars, thy breasts the milk'n way,
Thy fingers Cupid's shafts, thy voice the angels' lay:
And all I said so well, as no man it denied.

But now that hope is lost, unkindness kills delight,
Yet thought and speech do live, though metamorphos'd quite:
For rage now rules the reins, which guided were by pleasure.
I think now of thy faults, who late thought of thy praise,
That speech falls now to blame, which did thy honour raise,
The same key op'n can, which can lock up a treasure.

Thou then whom partial heavens conspir'd in one to frame,
The proof of Beauty's worth, th'inheritrix of fame,
The mansion seat of bliss, and just excuse of lovers;
See now those feathers pluckt, wherewith thou flew most high:
See what clouds of reproach shall dark thy honour's sky,
Whose own fault casts him down, hardly high seat recovers.

And O my Muse, though oft you lull'd her in your lap,
And then, a heav'nly child, gave her ambrosian pap:
And to that brain of hers your hidd'nest gifts infused,
Since she disdaining me, doth you in me disdain:
Suffer not her to laugh, while both we suffer pain:
Princes in subjects wrong'd, must deem themselves abused.

Your client poor myself, shall Stella handle so?
Revenge, revenge, my Muse, defiance' trumpet blow:
Threat'n what may be done, yet do more than you threat'n.
Ah, my suit granted is, I feel my breast doth swell:
Now child, a lesson new you shall begin to spell:
Sweet babes must babies[†] have, but shrewd[†] girls must be beat'n.

Think now no more to hear of warm fine odour'd snow,
Nor blushing lilies, nor pearls' ruby-hidden row,
Nor of that golden sea, whose waves in curls are brok'n:
But of thy soul, so fraught with such ungratefulness,
As where thou soon mightst help, most faith doth most oppress,
Ungrateful who is call'd, the worst of evils is spok'n:

Yet worse than worst, I say thou art a thief, a thief?
Now God forbid. A thief, and of worst thieves the chief:
Thieves steal for need, and steal but goods, which pain recovers,
But thou rich in all joys, doest rob my joys from me,
Which cannot be restor'd by time nor industry:
Of foes the spoil is evil, far worse of constant lovers.

Yet gentle English thieves do rob, but will not slay;
Thou English murd'ring thief, wilt have hearts for thy prey:
The name of murd'rer now on thy fair forehead sitteth:
And even while I do speak, my death wounds bleeding be:
Which (I protest) proceed from only cruel thee,
Who may and will not save, murder in truth committeth.

But murder, private fault, seems but a toy to thee,
I lay then to thy charge unjustest tyranny,
If rule by force without all claim a tyran showeth,
For thou doest lord my heart, who am not born thy slave,
And which is worse, makes me most guiltless torments have,
A rightful prince by unright deeds a tyran groweth.

Lo you grow proud with this, for tyrans make folk bow:
Of foul rebellion then I do appeach† thee now;
Rebel by Nature's law, rebel by law of reason,
Thou, sweetest subject, wert born in the realm of Love,
And yet against thy prince thy force dost daily prove:
No virtue merits praise, once toucht with blot of treason.

But valiant rebels oft in fools' mouths purchase fame:
I now then stain thy white with vagabonding shame,
Both rebel to the son, and vagrant from the mother;
For wearing Venus' badge, in every part of thee,
Unto Diana's train thou runaway didst flee:
Who faileth one, is false, though trusty to another.

What is not this enough? nay far worse cometh here;
A witch I say thou art, though thou so fair appear;
For I protest, my sight never thy face enjoyeth,
But I in me am chang'd, I am alive and dead:
My feet are turn'd to roots, my heart becometh lead,
No witchcraft is so evil, as which man's mind destroyeth.

Yet witches may repent, thou art far worse than they,
Alas that I am forc'd such evil of thee to say,
I say thou art a devil, though cloth'd in angel's shining:
For thy face tempts my soul to leave the heav'n for thee,
And thy words of refuse, do pour even hell on me:
Who tempt, and tempted plague, are devils in true defining.

You then ungrateful thief, you murd'ring tyran you,
You rebel run away, to lord and lady untrue,
You witch, you divill (alas) you still of me beloved,
You see what I can say; mend yet your froward mind,
And such skill in my Muse you reconcil'd shall find,
That all these cruel words your praises shall be proved.

babies dolls; *shrewd* shrewish; *appeach* impeach

Sixth song

O you that hear this voice,
O you that see this face,
Say whether† of the choice
Deserves the former place†:
Fear not to judge this bate†,
For it is void of hate.

This side doth beauty take,
For that doth music speak,
Fit orators to make
The strongest judgements weak:
The bar to plead their right,
Is only true delight.

Thus doth the voice and face,
These gentle lawyers wage,
Like loving brothers' case,
For father's heritage:
That each, while each contends,
Itself to other lends.

For beauty beautifies,
With heavenly hue and grace,
The heavenly harmonies;
And in this faultless face,
The perfect beauties be
A perfect harmony.

Music more loft'ly swells
In speeches nobly placed:
Beauty as far excels,
In action aptly graced:
A friend each party draws,
To countenance his cause:

Love more affected seems
To beauty's lovely light,
And wonder more esteems
Of music's wondrous might:
But both to both so bent,
As both in both are spent.

Music doth witness call
The ear, his truth to try:
Beauty brings to the hall,
The judgement of the eye,
Both in their objects such,
As no exceptions† touch.

The common sense, which might
Be arbiter of this,
To be forsooth upright,
To both sides partial is:
He lays on this chief praise,
Chief praise on that he lays.

The reason, Princess high,
Whose throne is in the mind,
Which music can in sky
And hidden beauties find,
Say whether thou wilt crown,
With limitless renown.

whether which; *former place* precedence; *bate* dispute; *exceptions* legal objections

Seventh song

Whose senses in so evil consort, their stepdame nature lays,
That ravishing delight in them most sweet tunes do not raise;
Or if they do delight therein, yet are so cloyed with wit,
As with sententious lips to set a title vain on it:
O let them hear these sacred tunes, and learn in wonder's schools,
To be (in things past bounds of wit) fools, if they be not fools.

Who have so leaden eyes, as not to see sweet beauty's show,
Or seeing, have so wodden wits, as not that worth to know;
Or knowing, have so muddy minds, as not to be in love;
Or loving, have so frothy thoughts, as eas'ly thence to move:
O let them see these heavenly beams, and in fair letters read
A lesson fit, both sight and skill, love and firm love to breed.

Hear then, but then with wonder hear; see but adoring see,
No mortal gifts, no earthly fruits, now here descended be:
See, do you see this face? a face? nay image of the skies,
Of which the two life-giving lights are figured in her eyes:
Hear you this soul-invading voice, and count it but a voice?
The very essence of their tunes, when angels do rejoice.

Eighth song

In a grove most rich of shade,
Where birds wanton music made,
May then young, his pied weeds showing,
New perfumed with fresh flowers growing,

Astrophil with Stella sweet,
Did for mutual comfort meet,
Both within themselves oppressed,
But each in the other blessed.

Him great harms had taught much care,
Her fair neck a foul yoke bare,
But her sight his cares did banish,
In his sight her yoke did vanish.

Wept they had, alas the while,
But now tears themselves did smile,
While their eyes by love directed,
Interchangeably reflected.

Sigh they did, but now betwixt
Sighs of woes were glad sighs mixt,
With arms cross'd, yet testifying
Restless rest, and living dying.

Their ears hungry of each word,
Which the dear tongue would afford,
But their tongues restrain'd from walking,
Till their hearts had ended talking.

But when their tongues could not speak,
Love itself did silence break;
Love did set his lips asunder,
Thus to speak in love and wonder:

"Stella, sovereign of my joy,
Fair triumpher of annoy,
Stella star of heavenly fire,
Stella loadstar of desire.

"Stella, in whose shining eyes,
Are the lights of Cupid's skies,
Whose beams where they once are darted,
Love therewith is straight imparted.

"Stella, whose voice when it speaks,
Senses all asunder breaks;
Stella, whose voice when it singeth,
Angels to acquaintance bringeth.

"Stella, in whose body is
Writ each character of bliss,
Whose face all, all beauty passeth,
Save thy mind which yet surpasseth.

"Grant, O grant, but speech alas,
Fails me fearing on to pass,
Grant, O me, what am I saying?
But no fault there is in praying.

"Grant, O dear, on knees I pray,
(Knees on ground he then did stay)
That not I, but since I love you,
Time and place for me may move you.

"Never season was more fit,
Never room more apt for it;
Smiling air allows my reason,
The birds sing: now use the season.

"This small wind which so sweet is,
See how it the leaves doth kiss,
Each tree in his best attiring,
Sense of love to love inspiring.

"Love makes earth the water drink,
Love to earth makes water sink;
And if dumb things be so witty,
Shall a heavenly grace want pity?"

There his hands in speech, fain
Would have made tongue's language plain;
But her hands his hands repelling,
Gave repulse all grace excelling.

Then she spake; her speech was such,
As not ears but heart did touch:
While such wise she love denied,
As yet love she signified.

"Astrophil", said she, "my love
Cease in these effects to prove:
Now be still, yet still believe me,
Thy grief more than death would grieve me.

"If that any thought in me,
Can taste comfort but of thee,
Let me, fed with hellish anguish,
Joyless, hopeless, endless languish.

"If those eyes you praised, be
Half so dear as you to me,
Let me home return, stark blinded
Of those eyes, and blinder minded.

"If to secret of my heart,
I do any wish impart,
Where thou art not foremost placed,
Be both wish and I defaced.

"If more may be said, I say,
All my bliss in thee I lay;
If thou love, my love content thee,
For all love, all faith is meant thee.

"Trust me while I thee deny,
In myself the smart I try,
Tyran honour doth thus use thee,
Stella's self might not refuse thee.

"Therefore, dear, this no more move,
Lest though I leave not thy love,
Which too deep in me is framed,
I should blush when thou art named."

Therewithall away she went,
Leaving him so passion rent,
With what she had done and spoken,
That therewith my song is broken.

Ninth song

Go my flock, go get you hence,
Seek a better place of feeding,
Where you may have some defence
From the storms in my breast breeding,
And showers from mine eyes proceeding.

Leave a wretch, in whom all woe
Can abide to keep no measure,
Merry flock, such one forgo,
Unto whom mirth is displeasure,
Only rich in mischief's treasure.

Yet alas before you go,
Hear your woeful master's story,
Which to stones I else would show:
Sorrowth only then hath glory,
When 'tis excellently sorry.

Stella fiercest shepherdess,
Fiercest but yet fairest ever;
Stella whom O heavens do bless,
Tho' against me she persever,
Tho' I bliss inherit never.

Stella hath refused me,
Stella who more love hath proved,
In this caitiff heart to be,
Than can in good ewes be moved
Toward lambkins best beloved.

Stella hath refused me,
Astrophil that so well served,
In this pleasant spring must see
While in pride flowers be preserved,
Himself only winter-sterved.

Why alas doth she then swear,
That she loveth me so dearly,
Seeing me so long to bear
Coals of love that burn so clearly;
And yet leave me helpless merely?

Is that love? forsooth I trow,
If I saw my good dog grieved,
And a help for him did know,
My love should not be believed,
But he were by me relieved.

No, she hates me, wellaway,
Feigning love, somewhat to please me:
For she knows, if she display
All her hate, death soon would seize me,
And of hideous torments ease me.

Then adieu, dear flock adieu:
But alas, if in your straying
Heavenly Stella meet with you,
Tell her in your piteous blaying,
Her poor slave's unjust decaying.

87

When I was forc'd from Stella ever dear,
Stella food of my thoughts, heart of my heart,
Stella whose eyes make all my tempests clear,
By iron laws of duty to depart:
   Alas I found, that she with me did smart,
I saw that tears did in her eyes appear;
I saw that sighs her sweetest lips did part,
And her sad words my saddest sense did hear.
   For me, I wept to see pearls scattered so,
   I sigh'd her sighs, and wailed for her woe,
Yet swam in joy, such love in her was seen.
   Thus while th'effect most bitter was to me,
   And nothing than the cause more sweet could be,
I had been vext, if vext I had not been.

88

Out traitor absence, darest thou counsel me,
From my dear captainness to run away?
Because in brave array[†] here marcheth she[†],
That to win me, oft shows a present pay?[†]
   Is faith so weak? or is such force in thee?
When sun is hid, can stars such beams display?
Cannot heav'ns food, once felt, keep stomachs free
From base desire on earthly cates[†] to prey?
   Tush absence, while thy mists eclipse that light,
   My orphan sense flies to the inward sight,
Where memory sets forth the beams of love.
   That where before heart loved and eyes did see,
   In heart both sight and love now coupled be;
United powers make each the stronger prove.

array dress/military order; *she* another woman; *shows...pay* offers immediate reward; *cates* food

Now that of absence the most irksome night,
  With darkest shade doth overcome my day;
  Since Stella's eyes, wont to give me my day,
Leaving my hemisphere, leave me in night,
Each day seems long, and longs for long-stay'd night,
  The night as tedious, woos th'approach of day;
  Tired with the dusty toils of busy day,
Languisht with horrors of the silent night;
Suffering the evils both of the day and night,
  While no night is more dark than is my day,
Nor no day hath less quiet than my night:
  With such bad mixture of my night and day,
That living thus in blackest winter night,
  I feel the flames of hottest summer day.

90

Stella think not that I by verse seek fame,
  Who seek, who hope, who love, who live but thee;
  Thine eyes my pride, thy lips my history:
If thou praise not, all other praise is shame.
Nor so ambitious am I, as to frame
  A nest for my young praise in laurel tree[†]:
  In truth I swear, I wish not there should be
Graved[†] in mine epitaph a poet's name:
  Ne if I would, could I just title make,
That any laud to me thereof should grow,
Without[†] my plumes from others' wings I take.
For nothing from my wit or will doth flow,
  Since all my words thy beauty doth indite,
  And love doth hold my hand, and makes me write.

laurel traditional reward of the poet; *graved* engraved/buried; *without* unless

Stella, while now by honour's cruel might,
   I am from you, light of my life mis-led,
   And that fair you my sun, thus overspred
With absence' veil, I live in sorrow's night.
If this dark place yet show like candle light,
   Some beauty's piece, as amber colour'd head,
   Milk hands, rose cheeks, or lips more sweet, more red,
Or seeing jets[†], black, but in blackness bright.
   They please I do confess, they please mine eyes,
But why? because of you they models be,
Models such be wood-globes[†] of glist'ring skies.
Dear, therefore be not jealous over me,
   If you hear that they seem my heart to move,
   Not them, O no, but you in them I love.

seeing jets eyes; *wood-globes* astronomical models

Be your words made (good sir) of Indian ware[†],
   That you allow me them by so small a rate?
   Or do you cutted Spartans[†] imitate,
Or do you mean my tender ears to spare?
That to my questions you so total[†] are,
   When I demand of phoenix Stella's state,
   You say forsooth, you left her well of late.
O God, think you that satisfies my care?
   I would know whether she did sit or walk,
How cloth'd, how waited on, sigh'd she or smil'd,
Whereof, with whom, how often did she talk,
With what pastime, time's journey she beguil'd,
   If her lips deign'd to sweeten my poor name,
   Say all, and all, well said, still say the same.

Indian ware i.e. rare, precious; *cutted* laconic; *total* brief

Tenth song

O dear life, when shall it be,
    That mine eyes thine eyes may see?
    And in them thy mind discover,
    Whether absence have had force
    Thy remembrance to divorce,
    From the image of thy lover?

O if I myself find not,
    After parting aught forgot,
    Nor debarr'd from beauty's treasure,
    Let no tongue aspire to tell,
    In what high joys I shall dwell,
    Only thought aims at the pleasure.

Thought therefore I will send thee,
    To take up the place for me;
    Long I will not after tarry,
    There unseen thou may'st be bold,
    Those fair wonders to behold,
    Which in them my hopes do carry.

Thought see thou no place forbear,
    Enter bravely everywhere,
    Seize on all to her belonging;
    But if thou wouldst guarded be,
    Fearing her beams, take with thee
    Strength of liking, rage of longing.

Think of that most grateful time,
    When my leaping heart will climb,
    In my lips to have his biding,
    There those roses for to kiss,
    Which do breath a sug'red bliss,
    Opening rubies, pearls dividing.

Think of my most princely power,
   When I blessed shall devour,
   With my greedy licorous[†] senses,
   Beauty, music, sweetness, love
   While she doth against me prove
   Her strong darts, but weak defences.

Think, think of those dallyings,
   When with dovelike murmurings,
   With glad moaning passed anguish,
   We change eyes, and heart for heart,
   Each to other do impart,
   Joying till joy make us languish.

O my thoughts my thoughts surcease,
   Thy delights my woes increase,
   My life melts with too much thinking;
   Think no more but die in me,
   Till thou shalt revived be,
   At her lips my nectar drinking.

licorous fond of good things/lustful

93

O fate, O fault, O curse, child of my bliss,
   What sobs can give words grace my grief to show?
   What ink is black enough to paint my woe?
Through me, wretch me, even Stella vexed is.
Yet truth (if caitiff's breath might call thee) this
   Witness with me, that my foul stumbling so,
   From carelessness did in no manner grow,
But wit confus'd with too much care did miss[†].
   And do I then myself this vain 'scuse give?
I have (live I and know this) harmed thee,
Tho' worlds quite[†] me, shall I myself forgive?
Only with pains my pains thus eased be,

That all thy hurts in my heart's wrack I read;
I cry thy sighs; my dear, thy tears I bleed.

miss fail to understand; *quite* acquit

94

Grief find the words, for thou hast made my brain
    So dark with misty vapours, which arise
    From out thy heavy mould, that inbent eyes
Can scarce discern the shape of mine own pain.
Do thou then (for thou canst) do thou complain,
    For my poor soul, which now that sickness tries,
    Which even to sense, sense of itself denies,
Though harbingers of death lodge there his train.
    Or if thy love of plaint yet mine forbears,
As of a caitiff worthy so to die,
Yet wail thyself, and wail with causeful tears,
That though in wretchedness thy life doth lie,
Yet growest more wretched than thy nature bears,
By being placed in such a wretch as I.

95

Yet sighs, dear sighs, indeed true friends you are,
    That do not leave your left friend at the worst,
    But as you with my breast I oft have nurst,
So grateful now you wait upon my care.
Faint coward joy no longer tarry dare,
    Seeing hope yield when this woe strake him first:
    Delight protests he is not for the accurst,
Though oft himself my mate-in-arms he sware.
    Nay sorrow comes with such main rage, that he
Kills his own children, tears, finding that they
By love were made apt to consort with me.
Only true sighs, you do not go away,
    Thank may you have for such a thankful part,
    Thank-worthiest yet when you shall break my heart.

Thought with good cause thou likest so well the night,
   Since kind[†] or chance gives both one livery,
   Both sadly black, both blackly dark'ned be,
Night barr'd from sun, thou from thy own sun's light;
Silence in both displays his sullen might,
   Slow heaviness in both holds one degree[†],
   That full of doubts, thou of perplexity;
Thy tears express night's native moisture right.
   In both a mazeful[†] solitariness:
In night of sprites the ghastly powers stir,
In thee or sprites or sprited ghastliness:
But but (alas) night's side the odds hath fur[†],
   For that at length yet doth invite some rest,
   Thou though still tired, yet still dost it detest.

kind nature; *one degree* the same rank; *mazeful* bewildering; *fur* far

Dian that fain would cheer her friend the Night,
   Shows her oft at the full her fairest face,
   Bringing with her those starry nymphs, whose chase
From heavenly standing[†] hits each mortal wight.
But ah poor night, in love with Phoebus' light,
   And endlessly despairing of his grace,
   Herself (to show no other joy hath place)
Silent and sad in mourning weeds doth dight:
   Even so (alas) a lady Dian's peer,
With choice delights and rarest company,
Would fain drive clouds from out my heavy cheer.
But woe is me, though joy itself were she,
   She could not show my blind brain ways of joy,
   While I despair my sun's sight to enjoy.

standing hunting station

98

Ah bed, the field where joy's peace some do see,
  The field where all my thoughts to war be train'd,
  How is thy grace by my strange fortune stain'd!
How thy lee shores by my sighs stormed be!
With sweet soft shades thou oft invitest me
  To steal some rest, but wretch I am constrain'd,
  (Spurr'd with love's spur, though gall'd and shortly rein'd
With care's hard hand) to turn and toss in thee.
  While the black horrors of the silent night,
  Paint woe's black face so lively to my sight,
That tedious leisure marks each wrinkled line:
  But when Aurora leads out Phoebus' dance,
  Mine eyes then only wink†, for spite perchance,
That worms should have their sun, and I want mine.

wink close

99

When far spent night persuades each mortal eye,
  To whom nor art nor nature granteth light,
  To lay his then mark wanting† shafts of light,
Clos'd with their quivers in sleep's armory;
With windows ope then most my mind doth lie,
  Viewing the shape of darkness and delight,
  Takes in that sad hue, which with th'inward night
Of his maz'd powers keeps perfit harmony:
  But when birds charm†, and that sweet air, which is
Morn's messenger, with rose enamel'd skies
Calls each wight to salute the flower of bliss;
In tomb of lids then buried are mine eyes,
  Forc'd by their lord, who is asham'd to find
  Such light in sense, with such a dark'ned mind.

mark wanting targetless; *charm* sing in unison

100

O tears, no tears, but rain from beauty's skies,
  Making those lilies and those roses grow,
  Which aye most fair, now more than most fair show,
While graceful pity beauty beautifies.
O honied sighs, which from that breast do rise,
  Whose pants do make unspilling cream to flow,
  Wing'd with whose breath, so pleasing Zephyrs blow,
As can refresh the hell where my soul fries.
  O plaints conserv'd in such a sug'red phrase,
  That eloquence itself envies your praise,
While sobb'd out words a perfect music give.
  Such tears, sighs, plaints, no sorrow is, but joy:
  Or if such heavenly signs must prove[†] annoy,
All mirth farewell, let me in sorrow live.

prove signify

101

Stella is sick, and in that sickbed lies
Sweetness, that breathes and pants as oft as she:
And grace sick too, such fine conclusions tries,
That sickness brags itself best graced to be.
  Beauty is sick, but sick in so fair guise,
That in that paleness beauty's white we see,
And joy which is inseparate from those eyes,
Stella now learns (strange case) to weep in thee.
  Love moves thy pain, and like a faithful page
As thy looks stir, runs up and down to make
All folks press'd at thy will thy pain to 'suage,
Nature with care sweats for her darling's sake,
  Knowing worlds pass, ere she enough can find
  Of such heaven stuff, to clothe so heavenly mind.

Where be those roses gone, which sweet'ned so our eyes?
    Where those red cheeks, which oft with fair increase[†] did frame
    The height of honour in the kindly badge of shame?
Who hath the crimson weeds stol'n from my morning skies?
How doth the colour vade[†] of those vermillion dies,
    Which Nature' self did make, and self engrain'd[†] the same?
    I would know by what right this paleness overcame
That hue, whose force my heart still unto thralldom ties?
    Galen's adoptive sons[†], who by a beaten way
    Their judgements hackney on, the fault on sickness lay,
But feeling proof makes me say they mistake it fur[†]:
    It is but love, which makes his paper perfit white
    To write therein more fresh the story of delight,
While beauty's reddest ink Venus for him doth stir.

fair increase i.e. blushing; *vade* fade; *engrain'd* dyed; *Galen's...sons* followers of Galen, old-fashioned physicians; *fur* far

O happy Thames, that didst my Stella bear,
I saw thyself with many a smiling line
Upon thy cheerful face, joy's livery wear:
While those fair planets on thy streams did shine.
    The boat for joy could not to dance forbear,
While wanton winds with beauties so divine
Ravisht, stay'd not, till in her golden hair
They did themselves (O sweetest prison) twine.
    And fain those Aeols' youths[†] there would their stay
Have made, but forc'd by Nature still to fly,
First did with puffing kiss those locks display:
She so dishevell'd, blusht; from window I
    With sight thereof cried out; O fair disgrace,
    Let honour' self to thee grant highest place.

Aeols' youths breezes

Envious wits what hath been mine offence,
    That with such poisonous care my looks you mark,
    That to each word, nay sigh of mine you hark,
As grudging me my sorrow's eloquence?
Ah, is it not enough, that I am thence,
    Thence, so far thence, that scarcely any spark
    Of comfort dare come to this dungeon dark,
Where rigour's exile locks up all my sense?
    But if I by a happy window† pass,
If I but stars upon mine armour bear,
Sick, thirsty, glad (though but of empty glass:)
Your mortal notes straight my hid meaning tear
    From out my ribs, and puffing prove that I
    Do Stella love. Fools, who doth it deny?

happy i.e. graced by Stella

Eleventh song

"Who is it that this dark night,
Underneath my window plaineth?"
It is one who from thy sight,
Being (ah) exil'd, disdaineth
Every other vulgar light.

"Why alas, and are you he?
Be not yet those fancies changed?"
Dear when you find change in me,
Though from me you be estranged,
Let my change to ruin be.

"Well in absence this will die,
Leave to see, and leave to wonder."
Absence sure will help, if I
Can learn, how myself to sunder
From what in my heart doth lie.

"But time will these thoughts remove:
Time doth work what no man knoweth."
Time doth as the subject prove,
With time still th'affection groweth
In the faithful turtle dove.

"What if you new beauties see,
Will not they stir new affection?"
I will think they pictures be,
(Image like of saints' perfection)
Poorly counterfeiting thee.

"But your reason's purest light,
Bids you leave such minds to nourish."
Dear, do reason no such spite,
Never doth thy beauty flourish
More than in my reason's sight.

"But the wrongs love bears, will make
Love at length leave undertaking."
No, the more fools it do shake,
In a ground of so firm making,
Deeper still they drive the stake.

"Peace, I think that some give ear:
Come no more, lest I get anger."
Bliss, I will my bliss forbear,
Fearing (sweet) you to endanger,
But my soul shall harbour there.

"Well, be gone, be gone I say,
Lest that Argus eyes[†] perceive you."
O unjustest fortune's sway,
Which can make me thus to leave you,
And from louts to run away.

Argus many-eyed monster

105

Unhappy sight, and hath she vanisht by
 So near, in so good time, so free a place?
 Dead glass[t], dost thou thy object so embrace,
As what my heart still sees thou canst not spy?
I swear by her love and lack, that I
 Was not in fault, who bent thy dazzling race[t]
 Only unto the heav'n of Stella's face,
Counting but dust what in the way did lie.
 But cease mine eyes, your tears do witness well,
That you guiltless thereof, your nectar missed:
Curst be the page from whom the bad torch fell,
Curst be the night which did your strife resist,
 Curst be the coachman which did drive so fast,
 With no worse curse than absence makes me taste.

glass eye; *dazzling race* dazed view

106

O absent presence Stella is not here;
 False flattering hope, that with so fair a face,
 Bare me in hand[t], that in this orphan place,
Stella, I say my Stella, should appear.
What say'st thou now, where is that dainty cheer,
 Thou told'st mine eyes should help their famisht case?
 But thou art gone, now that self felt disgrace
Doth make me most to wish thy comfort near.
 But here I do store of fair ladies meet,
 Who may with charm of conversation sweet,
Make in my heavy mould[t] new thoughts to grow:
 Sure they prevail as much with me, as he
 That bade his friend, but then new maim'd, to be
Merry with him, and not think of his woe.

bare . . . hand delude; *mould* body

107

Stella since thou so right a princess art
  Of all the powers which life bestows on me
  That ere by them ought undertaken be,
They first resort unto that sovereign part;
Sweet, for a while give respite to my heart,
  Which pants as though it still should leap to thee:
  And on my thoughts give thy lieutenancy
To this great cause, which needs both use[†] and art.
  And as a queen, who from her presence sends
Whom she employs, dismiss from thee my wit,
Till it have wrought what thy own will attends.
On servants' shame oft master's blame doth sit;
  O let not fools in me thy works reprove,
  And scorning say, "See what it is to love."

use experience

108

When sorrow (using mine own fire's might)
  Melts down his lead into my boiling breast,
  Through that dark furnace to my heart oppresst,
There shines a joy from thee my only light;
But soon as thought of thee breeds my delight,
  And my young soul flutters to thee his nest,
  Most rude despair my daily unbidden guest,
Clips straight my wings, straight wraps me in his night,
  And makes me then bow down my head, and say,
Ah what doth Phoebus' gold that wretch avail,
Whom iron doors do keep from use of day?
So strangely (alas) thy works in me prevail,
  That in my woes for thee thou art my joy,
  And in my joys for thee my only annoy.

The Defence of Poesy

When the right virtuous Edward Wotton and I were at the Emperor's Court* together, we gave ourselves to learn horseman-ship of John Pietro Pugliano, one that with great commendation had the place of an esquire in his stable. And he, according to the fertileness of the Italian wit, did not only afford us the demon-stration of his practice, but sought to enrich our minds with the contemplations therein, which he thought most precious. But with none I remember mine ears were at any time more loaden, than when (either angered with slow payment, or moved with our learner-like admiration) he exercised his speech in the praise of his faculty. He said soldiers were the noblest estate of mankind, and horsemen the noblest of soldiers. He said they were the masters of war and ornaments of peace, speedy goers and strong abiders, triumphers both in camps and courts. Nay, to so un-believed a point he proceeded, as that no earthly thing bred such wonder to a prince as to be a good horseman. Skill of government was but a *pedanteria* [thing of pedantry] in comparison. Then would he add certain praises by telling what a peerless beast a horse was: the only serviceable courtier without flattery, the beast of most beauty, faithfulness, courage, and such more, that if I had not been a piece of a logician before I came to him, I think he would have persuaded me to have wished myself a horse.

But thus much at least with his no few words he drave into me, that self-love is better than any gilding to make that seem gorgeous wherein ourselves are parties. Wherein, if Pugliano's strong affection and weak arguments will not satisfy you, I will give you a nearer example of myself, who (I know not by what mischance) in these my not old years and idlest times, having slipped into the title of a poet, am provoked to say something unto you in the defence of that my unelected vocation, which if I handle with more good will than good reasons, bear with me, since the scholar is to be pardoned that followeth the steps of his master. And yet I must say that, as I have just cause to make a pitiful defence of poor Poetry, which from almost the highest estimation of learning is fallen to be the laughing-stock of children, so have I need to bring some more available [availing, effective] proofs; since the former [i.e. horsemanship] is by no man barred of his deserved credit, the silly latter hath had even the names of philosophers used to the defacing of it, with great danger of civil war among the Muses.

And first, truly, to all them that, professing learning, inveigh against Poetry, may justly be objected that they go very near to ungratefulness, to seek to deface that which, in the noblest nations and languages that are known, hath been the first light-giver to ignorance, and first nurse: whose milk by little and little enabled them to feed afterwards of tougher knowledges. And will they now play the hedgehog that, being received into the den, drave out his host? Or rather the vipers, that with their birth kill their parents? Let learned Greece, in any of her manifold sciences, be able to show me one book before Musaeus, Homer and Hesiod, all three nothing else but poets. Nay, let any history be brought that can say any writers were there before them, if they were not men of the same skill, as Orpheus, Linus, and some other are named; who, having been the first of that country that made pens deliverers of their knowledge to their posterity, may justly challenge to be called their fathers in learning. For not only in time they had this priority (although in itself antiquity be venerable) but went before them, as causes to draw with their charming [i.e. sung, incantatory] sweetness the wild untamed wits to an admiration of knowledge. So as Amphion was said to move stones with his poetry to build Thebes, and Orpheus to be listened to by beasts (indeed stony and beastly people): so, among the Romans were Livius Andronicus, and Ennius.* So in the Italian language the first that made it aspire to be a treasure-house of science [learning] were the poets, Dante, Boccaccio, and Petrarch. So in our English were Gower and Chaucer, after whom, encouraged and delighted with their excellent fore-going, others have followed, to beautify our mother tongue, as well in the same kind as in other arts.

This did so notably show itself, that the philosophers of Greece durst not a long time appear to the world but under the mask of poets. So Thales, Empedocles, and Parmenides sang their natural philosophy in verse; so did Pythagoras and Phocylides their moral counsels; so did Tyrtaeus in war matters, and Solon in matters of policy [government]:* or rather they, being poets, did exercise their delightful vein in those points of highest knowledge, which before them lay hidden to the world. For that wise Solon was directly a poet is manifest, having written in verse the notable fable of the Atlantic Island [*Atlantis*, in *Timaeus*], which was continued by Plato.

And truly even Plato, whosoever well considereth, shall find that in the body of his work, though the inside and strength were Philosophy, the skin as it were and beauty depended most of Poetry. For all stands upon dialogues wherein he feigns many honest burgesses of Athens to speak of such matters that, if they had been set on the rack, they would never have confessed them; besides his poetical describing the circumstances of their meetings, as the well ordering of a banquet [setting of the *Symposium*], the delicacy of a walk [setting of *Phaedrus*], with interlacing mere tales, as Gyges' Ring* and others, which who knoweth not to be flowers of Poetry did never walk into Apollo's garden.

And even historiographers (although their lips sound of things done, and verity be written in their foreheads) have been glad to borrow both fashion and perchance weight of poets. So Herodotus entitled his History* by the name of the nine Muses; and both he and all the rest that followed him either stole or usurped of Poetry their passionate describing of passions, the many particularities of battles, which no man could affirm, or, if that be denied me, long orations put in the mouths of great kings and captains, which it is certain they never pronounced.

So that, truly, neither philosopher nor historiographer could at the first have entered into the gates of popular judgements, if they had not taken a great passport of Poetry, which in all nations at this day, where learning flourisheth not, is plain to be seen; in all which they have some feeling of Poetry.

In Turkey, besides their law-giving divines, they have no other writers but poets. In our neighbour country, Ireland, where truly learning goeth very bare, yet are their poets held in a devout reverence. Even among the most barbarous and simple Indians where no writing is, yet have they their poets who make and sing songs, which they call *areytos*, both of their ancestors' deeds

104

and praises of their gods – a sufficient probability that, if ever learning come among them, it must be by having their hard dull wits softened and sharpened with the sweet delights of Poetry. For until they find a pleasure in the exercise of the mind, great promises of much knowledge will little persuade them, that know not the fruits of knowledge. In Wales, the true remnant of the ancient Britons, as there are good authorities to show the long time they had poets, which they call *bards*, so through all the conquests of Romans, Saxons, Danes, and Normans, some of whom did seek to ruin all memory of learning from among them, yet do their poets even to this day last. So as it is not more notable in the soon beginning than in long continuing.

But since the authors of most of our sciences were the Romans, and before them the Greeks, let us a little stand upon their authorities, but even so far as to see what names they have given unto this now scorned skill.

Among the Romans a poet was called *vates*, which is as much as a diviner, foreseer, or prophet, as by his conjoined words *vaticinium* [a prophecy] and *vaticinari* [to prophesy] is manifest: so heavenly a title did that excellent people bestow upon this heart-ravishing knowledge. And so far were they carried into the admiration thereof, that they thought in the chanceable hitting upon any such verses great fore-tokens of their following fortunes were placed. Whereupon grew the word of *Sortes Virgilianae*,* when by the sudden opening Virgil's book they lighted upon any verse of his making, as is reported by many. Whereof the Histories of the Emperors' Lives are full, as of Albinus,* the governor of our island, who in his childhood met with this verse: *Arma amens capio nec sat rationis in armis*: and in his age performed it: which although it were a very vain and godless superstition, as also it was to think spirits were commanded by such verses (whereupon this word "charms", derived of *carmina*, cometh), so yet serveth it to show the great reverence those wits were held in. And altogether not without ground, since both the oracles of Delphos and Sibylla's prophecies were wholly delivered in verse. For that same exquisite observing of number and measure in words, and that high-flying liberty of conceit [imagination] proper to the poet, did seem to have some divine force in it.

And may not I presume a little farther, to show the reasonableness of this word *vates*, and say that the holy David's Psalms are a divine poem? If I do, I shall not do it without the testimony of great learned men, both ancient and modern. But even the name, psalms, will speak for me, which being interpreted, is nothing but songs; then, that it is fully written in metre, as all learned Hebricians agree, although the rules be not yet fully found; lastly and principally, his handling his prophecy, which is merely [wholly] poetical. For what else is the awaking his musical instruments? the often and free changing of persons? his notable *prosopopeias* [personifications], when he maketh you, as it were, see God coming in His majesty? his telling of the beasts' joyfulness, and hills leaping? but a heavenly Poesy, wherein almost [indeed] he showeth himself a passionate lover of that unspeakable and everlasting beauty to be seen by the eyes of the mind, only cleared by faith? But truly now having named him, I fear I seem to prophane that holy name, applying it to Poetry, which is among us thrown down to so ridiculous an estimation. But they that with quiet judgements will look a little deeper into it, shall find the end and working of it such as, being rightly applied, deserveth not to be scourged out of the Church of God.

But now let us see how the Greeks named it, and how they deemed of it. The Greeks called him *poieten* [a poet], which name hath, as the most excellent, gone through other languages. It cometh of this word *poiein*, which is "to make": wherein, I know not whether by luck or wisdom, we Englishmen have met with the Greeks in calling him "a maker". Which name, how high and incomparable a title it is, I had rather were known by marking the scope of other sciences than by any partial [biased] allegation.

There is no art delivered to mankind that hath not the works of Nature for his principal object, without which they could not consist, and on which they so depend, as they become actors and players, as it were of what Nature will have set forth. So doth the astronomer look upon the stars and, by that he seeth, set down what order Nature hath taken therein. So do the geometrician and arithmetician in their diverse sorts of quantities. So doth the musician in times [rhythmic measure] tell you which by nature agree, which not. The natural philosopher thereon hath his name, and the moral philosopher standeth upon the natural virtues, vices, and passions of man; and "follow Nature", saith he, "therein, and thou shalt not err". The lawyer saith what men have determined; the historian what men have done. The grammarian speaketh only of the rules of speech; and the rhetorician and logician, considering what in Nature will soonest prove and persuade, thereon give artificial rules, which still are compassed within the circle of a question according to the proposed matter. The physician weigheth the nature of a man's body, and the nature of things helpful or hurtful unto it. And the metaphysic, though it be in the second and abstract notions, and therefore be counted supernatural, yet doth he indeed build upon the depth of Nature.

Only the poet, disdaining to be tied to any such subjection, lifted up with the vigour of his own invention, doth grow in effect into another nature, in making things either better than Nature bringeth forth, or, quite anew – forms such as never were in Nature, as the Heroes, Demigods, Cyclops, Chimeras, Furies, and such like; so as he goeth hand in hand with Nature, not enclosed within the narrow warrant of her gifts, but freely ranging only within the zodiac of his own wit. Nature never set forth the earth in so rich tapestry as divers poets have done; neither with so pleasant rivers, fruitful trees, sweet-smelling flowers, nor whatsoever else may make the too much loved earth more lovely. Her world is brazen,* the poets only deliver a golden.

But let those things alone, and go to man – for whom as the other things are, so it seemeth in him her uttermost cunning is employed – and know whether she have brought forth so true a lover as Theagenes, so constant a friend as Pylades, so valiant a man as Orlando, so right a prince as Xenophon's Cyrus, so excellent a man every way as Virgil's Aeneas.* Neither let this be jestingly conceived, because the works of the one be essential [real], the other in imitation or fiction; for every understanding knoweth the skill of each artificer standeth in that Idea or foreconceit of the work, and not in the work itself. And that the poet hath that *Idea* is manifest, by delivering them forth in such excellency as he hath imagined them. Which delivering forth also is not wholly imaginative [fanciful], as we are wont to say by them that build castles in the air; but so far substantially it worketh, not only to make a Cyrus, which had been but a particular excellency as Nature might have done, but to bestow a Cyrus upon the world to make many Cyruses, if they will learn aright why and how that maker made him.

Neither let it be deemed too saucy a comparison to balance the highest point of man's wit with the efficacy of Nature; but rather give right honour to the heavenly Maker of that maker, who having made man in His own likeness, set him beyond and over all the works of that second nature [i.e. physical nature]; which in nothing he showeth so much as in Poetry, when with the force of a divine breath [inspiration] he bringeth things forth far surpassing her doings, with no small argument to the incredulous of that first accursed fall of Adam – since our erected wit maketh us know what perfection is, and yet our infected will keepeth us from reaching unto it. But these arguments will by few be understood, and by fewer granted. Thus much (I hope) will be given me, that the Greeks with some probability of reason gave him the name above all names of learning.

Now let us go to a more ordinary opening of him, that the truth may be the more palpable: and so I hope, though we get not so unmatched a praise as the etymology of his names will grant, yet his very description, which no man will deny, shall not justly be barred from a principal commendation. Poesy therefore is an art of imitation, for so Aristotle termeth it in the word *mimesis* – that is to say, a representing, counterfeiting, or figuring forth (to speak metaphorically, a speaking picture), with this end, to teach and delight.

Of this have been three several kinds. The chief, both in antiquity and excellency, were they that did imitate the inconceivable excellencies of God. Such were David in his Psalms; Solomon in his Song of Songs, in his Ecclesiastes, and Proverbs; Moses and Deborah in their Hymns; and the writer of Job – which, beside other, the learned Emanuel Tremellius and Franciscus Junius do entitle the poetical part of the Scripture.* Against these none will speak that hath the Holy Ghost in due holy reverence. In this kind, though in a full wrong [i.e. non-Christian] divinity, were Orpheus, Amphion, Homer in his Hymns, and many other, both Greeks and Romans. And this poesy must be used by whosoever will follow St. James's counsel in singing psalms when they are merry, and I know is used with the fruit of comfort by some when, in sorrowful pangs of their death-bringing sins, they find the consolation of the never-leaving goodness.

The second kind is of them that deal with matters philosophical: either moral, as Tyrtaeus, Phocylides, and Cato; or natural, as Lucretius and Virgil's Georgics; or astronomical, as Manilius and Pontanus; or historical, as Lucan:* which who mislike, the fault is in their judgement quite out of taste, and not in the sweet food of sweetly uttered knowledge.

But because this second sort is wrapped within the fold of the proposed subject, and takes not the free course of his own invention, whether they properly be poets or no let grammarians dispute, and go to the third, indeed right poets, of whom chiefly this question ariseth. Betwixt whom and these second is such a kind of difference as betwixt the meaner sort of painters, who counterfeit only such faces as are set before them, and the more excellent, who having no law but wit, bestow that in colours upon you which is fittest for the eye to see: as the constant though lamenting look of Lucretia,* when she punished in herself another's fault; wherein he painteth not Lucretia whom he never saw, but painteth the outward beauty of such a virtue. For these third be they which most properly do imitate to teach and delight, and to imitate borrow nothing of what is, hath been, or shall be; but range, only reined with learned discretion, into the divine consideration of what may be and should be. These be they that, as the first and most noble sort may justly be termed *vates*, so these are waited on in the excellentest languages and best understandings, with the foredescribed name of poets; for these indeed do merely make to imitate, and imitate both to delight and teach: and delight to move men to take that goodness in hand, which without delight they would fly as from a stranger, and teach, to make them know that goodness whereunto they are moved: which being the noblest scope to which ever any learning was directed, yet want there not idle tongues to bark at them.

These be subdivided into sundry more special denominations. The most notable be the Heroic, Lyric, Tragic, Comic, Satiric,

Iambic, Elegiac, Pastoral, and certain others, some of these being termed according to the matter they deal with, some by the sort of verse they liked best to write in; for indeed the greatest part of poets have apparalled their poetical inventions in that numbrous [metrical] kind of writing which is called verse – indeed but apparalled, verse being but an ornament and no cause of Poetry, since there have been many most excellent poets that never versified, and now swarm many versifiers that need never answer to the name of poets. For Xenophon, who did imitate so excellently as to give us *effigiem justi imperii*, "the portraiture of a just empire", under the name of Cyrus (as Cicero saith of him), made therein an absolute heroical poem. So did Heliodorus in his sugared [sweetly refined] invention of that picture of love in Theagenes and Chariclea [in the *Aethiopica*]; and yet both these wrote in prose: which I speak to show it is not rhyming and versing that maketh a poet (no more than a long gown maketh an advocate, who though he pleaded in armour should be an advocate and no soldier). But it is that feigning notable images of virtues, vices, or what else, with that delightful teaching, which must be the right describing note to know a poet by, although indeed the senate of poets hath chosen verse as their fittest raiment, meaning, as in matter they passed all in all, so in manner to go beyond them: not speaking – table talk fashion or like men in a dream – words as they chanceably fall from the mouth, but peising [weighing] each syllable of each word by just proportion according to the dignity of the subject.

Now therefore it shall not be amiss to weigh this latter sort of Poetry by his works, and then by his parts, and if in neither of these anatomies he be condemnable, I hope we shall obtain a more favourable sentence [judgement]. This purifying of wit, this enriching of memory, enabling of judgement, and enlarging of conceit, which commonly we call learning, under what name soever it come forth, or to what immediate end soever it be directed, the final end is to lead and draw us to as high a perfection as our degenerate souls, made worse by their clay lodgings, can be capable of. This, according to the inclination of the man, bred many formed impressions. For some that thought this felicity principally to be gotten by knowledge, and no knowledge to be

so high and heavenly as acquaintance with the stars, gave themselves to Astronomy; others, persuading themselves to be demigods if they knew the causes of things, became natural and supernatural philosophers; some an admirable delight drew to Music;
and some the certainty of demonstration to the Mathematics. But
all, one and other, having this scope – to know, and by knowledge
to lift up the mind from the dungeon of the body to the enjoying
his own divine essence. But when by the balance of experience
it was found that the astronomer looking to the stars might fall
into a ditch, that the inquiring philosopher might be blind in
himself, and the mathematician might draw forth a straight line
with a crooked heart: then lo, did proof, the overruler of opinions,
make manifest that all these are but serving [subordinate] sciences,
which, as they have each a private end in themselves, so yet are
they all directed to the highest end of the mistress-knowledge,
by the Greeks called *architectonike*, which stands (as I think) in
the knowledge of a man's self, in the ethic and politic consideration, with the end of well-doing and not of well-knowing only
– even as the saddler's next end is to make a good saddle, but
his further end to serve a nobler faculty, which is horsemanship;
so the horseman's to soldiery, and the soldier not only to have
the skill, but to perform the practice of a soldier. So that, the
ending end of all earthly learning being virtuous action, those
skills that most serve to bring forth that have a most just title to
be princes over all the rest.

Wherein, if we can show, the poet is worthy to have it before
any other competitors; among whom principally to challenge it
step forth the moral philosophers, whom methinks I see coming
towards me with a sullen gravity, as though they could not abide
vice by daylight, rudely clothed for to witness outwardly their
contempt of outward things, with books in their hands against
glory, whereto they set their names, sophistically speaking
against subtlety, and angry with any man in whom they see the
foul fault of anger. These men casting largesse as they go of
definitions, divisions, and distinctions [processes of scholastic
logic], with a scornful interrogative do soberly ask whether it be
possible to find any path so ready to lead a man to virtue as that
which teacheth what virtue is – and teacheth it not only by deli-

111

vering forth his very being, his causes, and effects, but also by making known his enemy, vice, which must be destroyed, and his cumbersome servant, passion, which must be mastered, by showing the generalities that contains* it, and the specialities that are derived from it; lastly, by plain setting down how it extends itself out of the limits of a man's own little world to the government of families, and maintaining of public societies.

The historian scarcely gives leisure to the moralist to say so much, but that he, loaden with old mouse-eaten records, authorising himself (for the most part) upon other histories, whose greatest authorities are built upon the notable foundation of hear-say; having much ado to accord differing writers and to pick truth out of partiality; better acquainted with a thousand years ago than with the present age, and yet better knowing how this world goes than how his own wit runs; curious for antiquities and inquisitive of novelties; a wonder to young folks and a tyrant in table talk; denieth, in a great chafe, that any man for teaching of virtue and virtuous actions is comparable to him. "I am *testis temporum, lux veritatis, vita memoriae, magistra vitae, nuncia vetustatis.** The philosopher," saith he, "teacheth a disputative virtue, but I do an active. His virtue is excellent in the dangerless Academy of Plato, but mine showeth forth her honourable face in the battles of Marathon, Pharsalia, Poitiers, and Agincourt. He teacheth virtue by certain abstract considerations, but I only bid you follow the footing of them that have gone before you. Old-aged experience goeth beyond the fine-witted philosopher, but I give the experience of many ages. Lastly, if he make the song-book, I put the learner's hand to the lute; and if he be the guide, I am the light".

Then would he allege you innumerable examples, confirming story by story, how much the wisest senators and princes have been directed by the credit of history, as Brutus, Alphonsus of Aragon,* and who not, if need be? At length the long line of their disputation makes a point [full stop] in this, that the one giveth the precept, and the other the example.

Now whom shall we find (since the question standeth for the highest form in the school of learning) to be moderator? Truly, as me seemeth, the poet; and if not a moderator, even the man that ought to carry the title from them both, and much more from all other serving sciences. Therefore compare we the poet with the historian and with the moral philosopher; and if he go beyond them both, no other human skill can match him. For as for the divine, with all reverence it is ever to be excepted, not only for having his scope as far beyond any of these as eternity exceedeth a moment, but even for passing each of these in themselves. And for the lawyer, though *ius* [law] be the daughter of justice, the chief of virtues, yet because he seeks to make men good rather *formidine poena* than *virtutis amore;** or, to say righter, doth not endeavour to make men good, but that their evil hurt not others; having no care, so he be a good citizen, how bad a man he be: therefore, as our wickedness maketh him necessary, and necessity maketh him honourable, so is he not in the deepest truth to stand in rank with these who all endeavour to take naughtiness away and plant goodness even in the secretest cabinet of our souls. And these four are all that any way deal in that consideration of men's manners, which being the supreme knowledge, they that best breed it deserve the best commendation.

The philosopher therefore and the historian are they which would win the goal, the one by precept, the other by example. But both, not having both, do both halt. For the philosopher, setting down with thorny argument the bare rule, is so hard of utterance and so misty to be conceived, that one that hath no other guide but him shall wade in him till he be old before he shall find sufficient cause to be honest. For his knowledge standeth so upon the abstract and general, that happy is that man who may understand him, and more happy that can apply what he doth understand. On the other side, the historian wanting [lacking] the precept, is so tied, not to what should be but to what is, to the particular truth of things and not to the general reason of things, that his example draweth no necessary consequence, and therefore a less fruitful doctrine.

Now doth the peerless poet perform both: for whatsoever the philosopher saith should be done, he gives a perfect picture of it in someone by whom he presupposeth it was done, so as he coupleth the general notion with the particular example. A perfect picture I say, for he yieldeth to the powers of the mind an image of that whereof the philosopher bestoweth but a wordish description, which doth neither strike, pierce, nor possess the sight of the soul so much as that other doth. For as in outward things, to a man that had never seen an elephant or a rhinoceros, who [the man who] should tell him most exquisitely all their shapes, colour, bigness, and particular marks; or of a gorgeous palace, the architecture, with declaring the full beauties might well make the hearer able to repeat, as it were by rote, all he had heard, yet should never satisfy his inward conceits with being witness to itself of a true lively knowledge; but the same man, as soon as he might see those beasts well painted, or the house well in model, should straightways grow, without need of any description, to a judicial comprehending of them. So no doubt the philosopher with his learned definition – be it of virtues or vices, matters of public policy or private government – replenisheth the memory with many infallible grounds of wisdom, which, notwithstanding, lie dark before the imaginative and judging power, if they be not illuminated or figured forth by the speaking picture of Poesy.

Tully taketh much pains, and many times not without poetical helps, to make us know the force love of our country hath in us. Let us but hear old Anchises speaking in the midst of Troy's flames, or see Ulysses in the fulness of all Calypso's delights bewail his absence from barren and beggarly Ithaca. Anger, the Stoics said, was a short madness: let but Sophocles bring you Ajax on a stage, killing and whipping sheep and oxen, thinking them the army of Greeks, with their chieftains Agamemnon and Menelaus, and tell me if you have not a more familiar insight into anger than finding in the schoolmen his genus and difference. See whether wisdom and temperance in Ulysses and Diomedes, valour in Achilles, friendship in Nisus and Euryalus, even to an ignorant man carry not an apparent shining; and, contrarily, the remorse of conscience in Oedipus, the soon repenting pride in Agamemnon, the self-devouring cruelty in his father Atreus, the violence of ambition in the two Theban brothers, the sour-sweetness of revenge in Medea; and, to fall lower, the Terentian Gnatho and our Chaucer's Pandar so expressed that we now use their names to signify their trades; and finally, all virtues, vices, and passions so in their own natural states laid to the view,

114

that we seem not to hear of them, but clearly to see through them.*

But even in the most excellent determination of goodness, what philosopher's counsel can so readily direct a prince as the feigned Cyrus in Xenophon; or a virtuous man in all fortunes as Aeneas in Virgil; or a whole commonwealth as the way of Sir Thomas More's *Utopia*? I say the way, because where Sir Thomas More erred, it was the fault of the man and not of the poet, for that way of patterning a commonwealth was most absolute [perfect], though he perchance hath not so absolutely performed it. For the question is, whether the feigned image of Poetry or the regular instruction of philosophy hath the more force in teaching: wherein if the philosophers have more rightly showed themselves philosophers than the poets have attained to the high top of their profession, as in truth,

Mediocribus esse poetis,
Non dii, non homines, non concessere columnae;*

it is, I say again, not the fault of the art, but that by few men that art can be accomplished.

Certainly, even our Saviour Christ could as well have given the moral commonplaces of uncharitableness and humbleness as the divine narrative of Dives and Lazarus [Luke 16: 19-31]; or of disobedience and mercy, as that heavenly discourse of the lost child and the gracious father [Luke 15: 11-32]; but that His thorough-searching wisdom knew the estate of Dives burning in hell, and of Lazarus being in Abraham's bosom, would more constantly (as it were) inhabit both the memory and judgement. Truly, for myself, me seems I see before my eyes the lost child's disdainful prodigality, turned to envy a swine's dinner: which by the learned divines are thought not historical acts, but instructing parables.

For conclusion, I say the philosopher teacheth, but he teacheth obscurely, so as the learned only can understand him; that is to say, he teacheth them that are already taught. But the poet is the food for the tenderest stomachs; the poet is indeed the right popular philosopher, whereof Aesop's tales give good proof: whose pretty allegories, stealing under the formal tales of beasts, make many (more beastly than beasts) begin to hear the sound of virtue

115

from these dumb speakers.

But now may it be alleged that if this imagining of matters be so fit for the imagination, then must the historian needs surpass, who brings you images of true matters, such as indeed were done, and not such as fantastically or falsely may be suggested to have been done. Truly, Aristotle himself, in his discourse of poesy, plainly determineth this question, saying that Poetry is *philosophoteron* and *spoudaioteron*, that is to say, it is more philosophical and more studiously serious than history. His reason is, because poesy dealeth with *katholou*, that is to say with the universal consideration, and the history with *kathekaston*, the particular: "now," saith he, "the universal weighs what is fit to be said or done, either in likelihood or necessity (which the poesy considereth in his imposed names) and the particular only marks whether Alcibiades did, or suffered, this or that". Thus far Aristotle: which reason of his (as all his) is most full of reason.

For indeed, if the question were whether it were better to have a particular act truly or falsely set down, there is no doubt which is to be chosen, no more than whether you had rather have Vespasian's picture right as he was, or at the painter's pleasure, nothing resembling. But if the question be for your own use and learning, whether it be better to have it set down as it should be, or as it was, then certainly is more doctrinable [instructive] the feigned Cyrus in Xenophon than the true Cyrus in Justin, and the feigned Aeneas in Virgil than the right Aeneas in Dares Phrygius: as to a lady that desired to fashion her countenance to the best grace, a painter should more benefit her to portray a most sweet face, writing Canidia upon it, than to paint Canidia as she was, who Horace sweareth was foul and ill-favoured.*

If the poet do his part aright, he will show you in Tantalus, Atreus, and such like, nothing that is not to be shunned; in Cyrus, Aeneas, Ulysses, each thing to be followed; where the historian, bound to tell things as things were, cannot be liberal (without he will be poetical) of a perfect pattern, but, as in Alexander or Scipio himself, show doings, some to be liked, some to be misliked.* And then how will you discern what to follow but by your own discretion, which you had without reading Quintus Curtius? And whereas a man may say, though in universal consideration of doctrine the poet prevaileth, yet that the history, in his saying such a thing was done, doth warrant a man more in that he shall follow – the answer is manifest: that if he stand upon that *was* (as if he should argue, because it rained yesterday, therefore it should rain today) then indeed it hath some advantage to a gross conceit [crude understanding]. But if he know an example only informs a conjectured likelihood, and so go by reason, the poet doth so far exceed him as he is to frame his example to that which is most reasonable, be it in warlike, politic, or private matters; where the historian in his bare *was* hath many times that which we call fortune to overrule the best wisdom. Many times he must tell events whereof he can yield no cause; or if he do, it must be poetically.

For that a feigned example hath as much force to teach as a true example (for as for to move, it is clear, since the feigned may be tuned to the highest key of passion), let us take one example wherein an historian and a poet did concur. Herodotus and Justin do both testify that Zopyrus, King Darius' faithful servant, seeing his master long resisted by the rebellious Babylonians, feigned himself in extreme disgrace of his king; for verifying of which, he caused his own nose and ears to be cut off, and so flying to the Babylonians was received, and for his known valour so far credited, that he did find means to deliver them over to Darius. Much like matter doth Livy record of Tarquinius and his son. Xenophon excellently feigneth such another stratagem performed by Abradatas in Cyrus' behalf. Now would I fain know, if occasion be presented unto you to serve your prince by such an honest dissimulation, why you do not as well learn it of Xenophon's fiction as of the other's verity? And truly so much the better, as you shall save your nose by the bargain; for Abradatas did not counterfeit so far. So then the best of the historian is subject to the poet; for whatsoever action, or faction [course of conduct], whatsoever counsel, policy, or war stratagem the historian is bound to recite, that may the poet (if he list) with his imitation make his own, beautifying it both for further teaching, and more delighting, as it please him – having all, from Dante's heaven to his hell, under the authority of his pen. Which if I be asked what poets have done so, as I might well name some, yet say I and say again, I speak of the art, and not of the artificer.

Now, to that which commonly is attributed to the praise of history, in respect of the notable learning is gotten by marking the success [outcome], as though therein a man should see virtue exalted and vice punished – truly that commendation is peculiar to Poetry, and far off from history. For indeed Poetry ever sets virtue so out in her best colours, making Fortune her well-waiting handmaid, that one must needs be enamoured of her. Well may you see Ulysses in a storm, and in other hard plights; but they are but exercises of patience and magnanimity, to make them shine the more in the near-following prosperity. And of the contrary part, if evil men come to the stage, they ever go out (as the tragedy writer [Euripides] answered to one that misliked the show of such persons) so manacled, as they little animate folks to follow them. But the historian, being captived to the truth of a foolish world, is many times a terror from well-doing, and an encouragement to unbridled wickedness.

For see we not valiant Miltiades rot in his fetters? the just Phocion and the accomplished Socrates put to death like traitors? the cruel Severus live prosperously? the excellent Severus miserably murdered? Sylla and Marius dying in their beds? Pompey and Cicero slain when they would have thought exile a happiness? See we not virtuous Cato driven to kill himself, and rebel Caesar so advanced that his name yet, after 1600 years, lasteth in the highest honour?* And mark but even Caesar's own words of the forenamed Sylla (who in that only did honestly, to put down his dishonest tyranny), *literas nescivit* [did not know his alphabet], as if want of learning caused him to do well. He meant it not by Poetry which, not content with earthly plagues, deviseth new punishments in hell for tyrants, nor yet by philosophy, which teacheth *occidendos esse* [(tyrants) are to be killed]; but no doubt by skill in history, for that indeed can afford you Cypselus, Periander, Phalaris, Dionysius, and I know not how many more of the same kennel, that speed well enough in their abominable injustice or usurpation. I conclude therefore that he excelleth History, not only in furnishing the mind with knowledge, but in setting it forward to that which deserves to be called and accounted good; which setting forward and moving to well-doing indeed setteth the laurel crown upon the poet as victorious, not only of the historian, but over the philosopher, howsoever in teaching it may be questionable.

For suppose it be granted (that which I suppose with great reason may be denied) that the philosopher, in respect of his methodical proceeding, doth teach more perfectly than the poet, yet I do think that no man is so much *philophilosophos* [a lover of philosophy] as to compare the philosopher in moving with the poet. And that moving is of a higher degree than teaching, it may by this appear, that it is well nigh both the cause and effect of teaching. For who will be taught, if he be not moved with desire to be taught? And what so much good doth that teaching bring forth (I speak still of moral doctrine) as that it moveth one to do that which it doth teach? For, as Aristotle saith, it is not *gnosis* [knowing] but *praxis* [doing] must be the fruit. And how *praxis* cannot be, without being moved to practise, it is no hard matter to consider.

The philosopher showeth you the way, he informeth you of the particularities, as well of the tediousness of the way, as of the pleasant lodging you shall have when your journey is ended, as of the many by-turnings that may divert you from your way. But this is to no man but to him that will read him, and read him with attentive studious painfulness [painstakingly]; which constant desire whosoever hath in him, hath already passed half the hardness of the way, and therefore is beholding to the philosopher but for the other half. Nay truly, learned men have learnedly thought that where once reason hath so much overmastered passion as that the mind hath a free desire to do well, the inward light each mind hath in itself is as good as a philosopher's book; since in Nature we know it is well to do well, and what is well and what is evil, although not in the words of art which philosophers bestow upon us; for out of natural conceit the philosophers drew it. But to be moved to do that which we know, or to be moved with desire to know, *hoc opus, hic labor est* ["This the toil, this the struggle is", *Aeneid* VI].

Now therein of all sciences (I speak still of human, but according to the human conceit) is our poet the monarch. For he doth not only show the way, but giveth so sweet a prospect into the way, as will entice any man to enter into it. Nay, he doth, as if your journey should lie through a fair vineyard, at the very first give you a cluster of grapes, that full of that taste, you may long to pass further. He beginneth not with obscure definitions, which must blur the margent with interpretations, and load the memory with doubtfulness; but he cometh to you with words set in delightful proportion, either accompanied with, or prepared for, the well enchanting skill of music; and with a tale forsooth he cometh unto you, with a tale which holdeth children from play, and old men from the chimney corner. And, pretending no more, doth intend the winning of the mind from wickedness to virtue: even as the child is often brought to take most wholesome things by hiding them in such other as have a pleasant taste; which, if one should begin to tell them the nature of the aloes or rhubarb they should receive, would sooner take their physic at their ears than at their mouth. So is it in men (most of which are childish in the best things, till they be cradled in their graves): glad they will be to hear the tales of Hercules, Achilles, Cyrus and Aeneas, and, hearing them, must needs hear the right description of wisdom, valour and justice; which, if they had been barely (that is to say, philosophically) set out, they would swear they be brought to school again.

That imitation whereof Poetry is, hath the most conveniency to Nature of all other, insomuch that, as Aristotle saith, those things which in themselves are horrible, as cruel battles, unnatural monsters, are made in poetical imitation delightful. Truly, I have known men that, even with reading *Amadis de Gaule* [late medieval romance] (which God knoweth wanteth much of a perfect poesy), have found their hearts moved to the exercise of courtesy, liberality, and especially courage. Who readeth Aeneas carrying old Anchises on his back, that wisheth not it were his fortune to perform so excellent an act? Whom do not those words of Turnus move (the tale of Turnus having planted his image in the imagination)?

> Fugientem haec terra videbit?
> Usque adeone mori miserum est?*

Where the philosophers, as they scorn to delight, so must they be content little to move – saving wrangling whether virtue be the chief or the only good, whether the contemplative or the active life do excel – which Plato and Boethius well knew, and therefore made mistress Philosophy very often borrow the masking raiment of Poesy. For even those hard-hearted evil men who think virtue a school name, and know no other good but *indulgere genio* [follow their own devices], and therefore despise the austere admonitions of the philosopher, and feel not the inward reason they stand upon, yet will be content to be delighted – which is all the good-fellow [friend/thief] poet seems to promise – and so steal to see the form of goodness (which seen, they cannot but love) ere themselves be aware, as if they took a medicine of cherries.

Infinite proofs of the strange effects of this poetical invention might be alleged; only two shall serve, which are so often remembered as I think all men know them. The one of Menenius Agrippa who, when the whole people of Rome had resolutely divided themselves from the Senate, with apparent show of utter ruin, though he were (for that time) an excellent orator, came not among them upon trust of figurative speeches or cunning insinuations, and much less with farfetched maxims of philosophy, which (especially if they were Platonic) they must have learned geometry before they could well have conceived; but forsooth he behaves himself like a homely and familiar poet. He telleth them a tale, that there was a time when all the parts of the body made a mutinous conspiracy against the belly, which they thought devoured the fruits of each other's labour; they concluded they would let so unprofitable a spender starve. In the end, to be short (for the tale is notorious, and as notorious that it was a tale), with punishing the belly they plagued themselves. This applied by him wrought such effect in the people, as I never read that ever words brought forth but then so sudden and so good an alteration; for upon reasonable conditions a perfect reconcilement ensued. The other is of Nathan the prophet who, when the holy David had so far forsaken God as to confirm adultery with murder, when he was to do the tenderest offices of a friend in laying his own shame before his eyes, sent by God to call again so chosen a servant, how doth he it but by telling of a man whose beloved lamb was ungratefully taken from his bosom? The application most divinely true, but the discourse itself feigned; which made David (I speak of the second and instrumental cause) as in a glass see his own filthiness, as that heavenly psalm of mercy [Psalm 51] well testifieth.

By these, therefore, examples and reasons, I think it may be manifest that the poet, with that same hand of delight, doth draw the mind more effectually than any other art doth. And so a conclusion not unfitly ensueth: that, as virtue is the most excellent resting place for all worldly learning to make his end of, so Poetry – being the most familiar to teach it, and most princely to move towards it – in the most excellent work is the most excellent workman.

But I am content not only to decipher him by his works (although works in commendation or dispraise must ever hold an high authority), but more narrowly will examine his parts; so that, as in a man, though all together may carry a presence full of majesty and beauty, perchance in some one defectious piece we may find a blemish. Now in his parts, kinds, or species (as you list to term them), it is to be noted that some poesies have coupled together two or three kinds, as the tragical and comical, whereupon is risen the tragicomical. Some in the like manner have mingled prose and verse, as Sannazzaro and Boethius.* Some have mingled matters heroical and pastoral. But that cometh all to one in this question for, if severed they be good, the conjunction cannot be hurtful. Therefore, perchance forgetting some and leaving some as needless to be remembered, it shall not be amiss in a word to cite the special kinds, to see what faults may be found in the right use of them.

Is it then the Pastoral poem which is misliked? For perchance where the hedge is lowest [i.e. having the humblest style] they will soonest leap over. Is the poor pipe disdained, which sometime out of Meliboeus' mouth* can show the misery of people under hard lords or ravening soldiers? And again, by Tityrus, what blessedness is derived to them that lie lowest from the goodness of them that sit highest; sometimes, under the pretty tales of wolves and sheep, can include the whole considerations of wrong-doing and patience; sometimes show that contentions for trifles can get but a trifling victory – where perchance a man may see that even Alexander and Darius, when they strave who should be cock of this world's dunghill, the benefit they got was that the afterlivers may say:

> Haec memini et victum frustra contendere Thirsin:
> Ex illo Corydon, Corydon est tempore nobis.*

Or is it the lamenting Elegiac, which in a kind heart would move rather pity than blame, who bewails with the great philosopher Heraclitus the weakness of mankind and the wretchedness of the world? Who surely is to be praised, either for compassionate accompanying just causes of lamentation, or for rightly pointing out how weak be the passions of woefulness. Is it the bitter but wholesome Iambic [pointed satire, lampoon], which rubs the galled mind, in making shame the trumpet of villainy with bold and open crying out against naughtiness? Or the Satiric? who *Omne vafer vitium ridenti tangit amico;** who sportingly never leaveth till he make a man laugh at folly, and at length ashamed to laugh at himself – which he cannot avoid, without avoiding the folly; who, while *circum praecordia ludit,** giveth us to feel how many headaches a passionate life bringeth us to; how, when all is done, *Est Ulubris, animus si nos non deficit aequus.** No, perchance it is the Comic, whom naughty play-makers and stage-keepers have justly made odious. To the arguments of abuse I will answer after. Only thus much now is to be said, that the Comedy is an imitation of the common errors of our life, which he representeth in the most ridiculous and scornful sort that may be, so as it is impossible that any beholder can be content to be such a one.

Now, as in geometry the oblique must be known as well as the right, and in arithmetic the odd as well as the even, so in the actions of our life who seeth not the filthiness of evil wanteth a great foil to perceive the beauty of virtue. This doth the Comedy handle so in our private and domestical matters, as with hearing it we get as it were an experience, what is to be looked for of a niggardly Demea, of a crafty Davus, of a flattering Gnatho, of a vainglorious Thraso [characters from Terence]; and not only to know what effects are to be expected, but to know who be such by the signifying badge given them by the comedian. And little reason hath any man to say that men learn evil by seeing it so set out; since, as I said before, there is no man living but, by the force truth hath in Nature, no sooner seeth these men play their parts but wisheth them *in pistrinum* [in the mill for punishment] – although perchance the sack of his own faults lie so behind his back that he seeth not himself to dance the same measure; whereto yet nothing can more open his eyes than to find his own actions contemptibly set forth.

So that the right use of Comedy will, I think, by nobody be blamed, and much less of the high and excellent Tragedy, that openeth the greatest wounds, and showeth forth the ulcers that are covered with tissue; that maketh kings fear to be tyrants, and tyrants manifest their tyrannical humours; that, with stirring the affects [feelings] of admiration and commiseration, teacheth the uncertainty of this world, and upon how weak foundations gilden roofs are builded; that maketh us know,

> Qui sceptra saevus duro imperio regit,
> Timet timentes, metus in auctorem redit.*

But how much it can move, Plutarch yieldeth a notable testimony of the abominable tyrant Alexander Pheraeus, from whose eyes a tragedy, well made and represented, drew abundance of tears, who without all pity had murdered infinite numbers, and some of his own blood; so as he that was not ashamed to make matters for tragedies, yet could not resist the sweet violence of a tragedy. And if it wrought no further good in him, it was that he, in despite of himself, withdrew himself from hearkening to that which might mollify his hardened heart. But it is not the Tragedy they do mislike; for it were too absurd to cast out so excellent a representation of whatsoever is most worthy to be learned.

Is it the Lyric that most displeaseth, who with his tuned lyre and well-accorded [harmonized] voice, giveth praise, the reward of virtue, to virtuous acts; who gives moral precepts and natural problems [i.e. for logical analysis; see *Astrophil and Stella*, 3]; who sometimes raiseth up his voice to the height of the heavens, in singing the lauds of the immortal God? Certainly, I must confess my own barbarousness, I never heard the old song of Percy and Douglas [probably "Chevy Chase"] that I found not my heart moved more than with a trumpet; and yet is it sung but by some blind crowder [player of a "crowd", an old Celtic fiddle], with no rougher voice than rude style; which, being so evil apparelled in the dust and cobwebs of that uncivil age, what would it work trimmed in the gorgeous eloquence of Pindar? In Hungary I have seen it the manner at all feasts, and other such meetings, to have songs of their ancestors' valour, which that right soldierlike nation think one of the chiefest kindlers of brave courage. The incomparable Lacedemonians did not only carry that kind of music ever with them to the field, but even at home, as such songs were made, so were they all content to be singers of them – when the lusty men were to tell what they did, the old men what they had done, and the young what they would do. And where a man may say that Pindar many times praiseth highly victories of small moment, matters rather of sport [i.e. the Olympic Games] than virtue; as it may be answered, it was the fault of the poet and not of the poetry, so indeed the chief fault was in the time and custom of the Greeks, who set those toys at so high a price that Philip of Macedon reckoned a horserace won at Olympus among his three fearful felicities. But as the unimitable Pindar often did, so is that kind [i.e. the Lyric] most capable and most fit to awake the thoughts from the sleep of idleness, to embrace honourable enterprises.

There rests the Heroical, whose very name (I think) should daunt all back-biters. For by what conceit can a tongue be directed to speak evil of that which draweth with it no less champions than Achilles, Cyrus, Aeneas, Turnus, Tydeus and Rinaldo?* who doth not only teach and move to a truth, but teacheth and moveth to the most high and excellent truth; who maketh magnanimity and justice shine through all misty fearfulness and foggy desires; who, if the saying of Plato and Tully be true, that who could see virtue would be wonderfully ravished with the love of her beauty – this man sets her out to make her more lovely in her holiday apparel, to the eye of any that will deign not to disdain until they understand. But if anything be already said in defence of sweet Poetry, all concurreth to the maintaining the

Heroical, which is not only a kind, but the best and most accomplished kind of Poetry. For as the image of each action stirreth and instructeth the mind, so the lofty image of such worthies most inflameth the mind with desire to be worthy, and informs with counsel how to be worthy. Only let Aeneas be worn in the tablet of your memory, how he governeth himself in the ruin of his country; in the preserving of his old father, and carrying away his religious ceremonies [ceremonial objects]; in obeying the god's commandment to leave Dido, though not only all passionate kindness, but even the human consideration of virtuous gratefulness, would have craved other of him; how in storms, how in sports, how in war, how in peace, how a fugitive, how victorious, how besieged, how besieging, how to strangers, how to allies, how to enemies, how to his own; lastly, how in his inward self, and how in his outward government; and I think, in a mind not prejudiced with prejudicating humour, he will be found in excellency fruitful, yea, as Horace saith, *melius Chrysippo et Crantore.**

But truly I imagine it falleth out with these poet-whippers, as with some good women, who often are sick, but in faith they cannot tell where. So the name of Poetry is odious to them, but neither his cause nor effects, neither the sum that contains him, nor the particularities descending from him, give any fast [firm] handle to their carping dispraise.

Since then Poetry is of all human learning the most ancient and of most fatherly antiquity, as from whence other learnings have taken their beginnings; since it is so universal that no learned nation doth despise it, nor barbarous nation is without it; since both Roman and Greek gave such divine names unto it, the one of "prophesying", the other of "making", and that indeed that name of "making" is fit for him, considering that whereas other arts retain themselves within their subject, and receive (as it were) their being from it, the poet only bringeth his own stuff, and doth not learn a conceit out of a matter, but maketh matter for a conceit; since neither his description nor his end containeth any evil, the thing described cannot be evil; since his effects be so good as to teach goodness and delight the learners of it; since therein (namely in moral doctrine, the chief of all knowledges) he doth not only far pass the historian but, for instructing, is well nigh comparable to the philosopher, and, for moving, leaves him behind him; since the Holy Scripture (wherein there is no uncleanness) hath whole parts in it poetical, and that even our Saviour Christ vouchsafed to use the flowers of it; since all his kinds are not only in their united forms but in their severed dissections fully commendable; I think (and I think I think rightly) the laurel crown appointed for triumphant captains doth worthily, of all other learnings, honour the poet's triumph.

But because we have ears as well as tongues, and that the lightest reasons that may be will seem to weigh greatly if nothing be put in the counterbalance, let us hear, and as well as we can ponder, what objections may be made against this art, which may be worthy either of yielding or answering.

First, truly I note not only in these *mysomousoi*, poet-haters, but in all that kind of people who seek a praise by dispraising others, that they do prodigally spend a great many wandering words in quips and scoffs, carping and taunting at each thing which, by stirring the spleen, may stay the brain from a through-beholding the worthiness of the subject. Those kind of objections, as they are full of a very idle easiness, since there is nothing of so sacred a majesty but that an itching tongue may rub itself upon it, so deserve they no other answer but, instead of laughing at the jest, to laugh at the jester. We know a playing wit can praise the discretion of an ass, the comfortableness of being in debt, and the jolly commodities [advantages] of being sick of the plague. So of the contrary side, if we will turn Ovid's verse, *Ut lateat virtus proximitate mali*, that "good lie hid in nearness of the evil", Agrippa will be as merry in showing the vanity of science as Erasmus was in the commending of folly.* Neither shall any man or matter escape some touch of these smiling railers. But for Erasmus and Agrippa, they had another foundation than the superficial part would promise. Marry, these other pleasant fault-finders, who will correct the verb before they understand the noun, and confute others' knowledge before they confirm their own, I would have them only remember that scoffing cometh not of wisdom; so as the best title in true English they get with their merriments is to be called good fools, for so have our grave

127

forefathers ever termed that humorous kind of jesters.

But that which giveth greatest scope to their scorning humour is rhyming and versing. It is already said (and, as I think, truly said) it is not rhyming and versing that maketh Poesy. One may be a poet without versing, and a versifier without poetry. But yet presuppose it were inseparable (as indeed it seemeth Scaliger judgeth) truly it were an inseparable commendation. For if *oratio* next to *ratio*, speech next to reason, be the greatest gift bestowed upon mortality, that cannot be praiseless which doth most polish that blessing of speech; which considers each word not only (as a man may say) by his forcible quality, but by his best measured quantity, carrying even in themselves a harmony – without [unless], perchance, number, measure, order, proportion be in our time grown odious. But lay aside the just praise it hath, by being the only fit speech for Music (Music, I say, the most divine striker of the senses), thus much is undoubtedly true, that if reading be foolish without remembering, memory being the only treasurer of knowledge, those words which are fittest for memory are likewise most convenient for knowledge.

Now, that verse far exceedeth prose in the knitting up of the memory, the reason is manifest: the words (besides their delight, which hath a great affinity to memory) being so set as one cannot be lost but the whole work fails – which accusing itself [by breaking the metre], calleth the remembrance back to itself, and so most strongly confirmeth it. Besides, one word so (as it were) begetting another, as, be it in rhyme or measured verse, by the former a man shall have a near guess to the follower. Lastly, even they that have taught the art of memory have showed nothing so apt for it as a certain room divided into many places, well and thoroughly known. Now, that hath the verse in effect perfectly, every word having his natural seat, which seat must needs make the words remembered. But what needs more in a thing so known to all men? Who is it that ever was a scholar that doth not carry away some verses of Virgil, Horace, or Cato, which in his youth he learned, and even to his old age serve him for hourly lessons? – as

Percontatorem fugito, nam garrulus idem est.

Dum sibi quisque placet, credula turba sumus.*

128

But the fitness it hath for memory is notably proved by all delivery of arts; wherein for the most part, from Grammar to Logic, Mathematic, Physic, and the rest, the rules chiefly necessary to be borne away are compiled in verses. So that verse being in itself sweet and orderly, and being best for memory, the only handle of knowledge, it must be in jest that any man can speak against it.

Now then go we to the most important imputations laid to the poor poets. For aught I can yet learn, they are these. First, that there being many other more fruitful knowledges, a man might better spend his time in them than in this. Secondly, that it is the mother of lies. Thirdly, that it is the nurse of abuse, infecting us with many pestilent desires, with a siren's sweetness drawing the mind to the serpent's tale of sinful fancy – and herein, especially, comedies give the largest field to ear [plough] (as Chaucer saith); how both in other nations and in ours, before poets did soften us, we were full of courage, given to martial exercises, the pillars of manlike liberty, and not lulled asleep in shady idleness with poets' pastimes. And lastly, and chiefly, they cry out with an open mouth as if they had outshot Robin Hood, that Plato banished them out of his commonwealth. Truly, this is much, if there be much truth in it.

First, to the first, that a man might better spend his time is a reason indeed; but it doth (as they say) but *petere principium* [beg the question]: for if it be, as I affirm, that no learning is good as that which teacheth and moveth to virtue, and that none can both teach and move thereto so much as Poetry, then is the conclusion manifest that ink and paper cannot be to a more profitable purpose employed. And certainly, though a man should grant their first assumption, it should follow (methinks) very unwillingly, that good is not good because better is better. But I still and utterly deny that there is sprung out of earth a more fruitful knowledge.

To the second therefore, that they should be the principal liars, I answer paradoxically but truly, I think truly, that of all writers under the sun the poet is the least liar, and, though he would, as a poet can scarcely be a liar. The astronomer, with his cousin the geometrician, can hardly escape, when they take upon them to measure the height of the stars. How often, think you, do the physicians lie, when they aver things good for sicknesses, which afterwards send Charon [ferrier of the dead across the Styx] a great number of souls drowned in a potion before they come to his ferry? And no less of the rest, which take upon them to affirm. Now for the poet, he nothing affirms, and therefore never lieth. For, as I take it, to lie is to affirm that to be true which is false; so as the other artists [liberal arts], and especially the historian, affirming many things, can, in the cloudy knowledge of mankind, hardly escape from many lies. But the poet (as I said before) never affirmeth. The poet never maketh any circles [such as circumscribe a magician's power] about your imagination, to conjure you to believe for true what he writes. He citeth not authorities of other histories, but even for his entry [opening] calleth the sweet Muses to inspire into him a good invention; in truth, not labouring to tell you what is or is not, but what should or should not be. And therefore, though he recount things not true, yet because he telleth them not for true, he lieth not – without we will say that Nathan lied in his speech before-alleged to David; which as a wicked man durst scarce say, so think I none so simple would say that Aesop lied in the tales of his beasts; for who thinks that Aesop writ it for actually true were well worthy to have his name chronicled among the beasts he writeth of. What child is there that, coming to a play, and seeing *Thebes* written in great letters upon an old door, doth believe that it is Thebes? If then a man can arrive, at that child's age, to know that the poets' persons and doings are but pictures of what should be, and not stories what have been, they will never give the lie to things not affirmatively but allegorically and figuratively written. And therefore, as in History looking for truth, they may go away full fraught with falsehood, so in Poesy looking but for fiction, they shall use the narration but as an imaginative ground-plot of a profitable invention.

But hereto is replied, that the poets give names to men they write of, which argueth a conceit of an actual truth, and so, not being true, proves a falsehood. And doth the lawyer lie then, when under the names of "John of the Stile" and "John of the Noakes" he puts his case? But that is easily answered. Their naming of men is but to make their picture the more lively, and not to build any history: painting men, they cannot leave men nameless.

We see we cannot play at chess but that we must give names to our chessmen; and yet, methinks, he were a very partial champion of truth that would say we lied for giving a piece of wood the reverend title of a bishop. The poet nameth Cyrus and Aeneas no other way than to show what men of their fames, fortunes, and estates should do.

Their third is, how much it abuseth men's wit, training it to wanton sinfulness and lustful love; for indeed that is principal, if not the only, abuse I can hear alleged. They say the Comedies rather teach than reprehend amorous conceits. They say the Lyric is larded with passionate sonnets, the Elegiac weeps the want of his mistress, and that even to the Heroical Cupid hath ambitiously climbed. Alas, Love, I would thou couldst as well defend thyself as thou canst offend others. I would those on whom thou dost attend could either put thee away, or yield good reason why they keep thee. But grant love of beauty to be a beastly fault (although it be very hard, since only man, and no beast, hath that gift to discern beauty); grant that lovely name of Love to deserve all hateful reproaches (although even some of my masters the philosophers spent a good deal of their lamp-oil in setting forth the excellency of it); grant, I say, whatsoever they will have granted, that not only love, but lust, but vanity, but – if they list – scurrility possesseth many leaves of the poets' books; yet think I, when this is granted, they will find their sentence may with good manners put the last words foremost, and not say that Poetry abuseth man's wit, but that man's wit abuseth Poetry.

For I will not deny but that man's wit may make Poesy, which should be *eikastike* [imitative], which some learned have defined, "figuring forth good things", to be *phantastike* [fantastic], which doth contrariwise infect the fancy with unworthy objects; as the painter – that should give to the eye either some excellent perspective, or some fine picture, fit for building or fortification, or containing in it some notable example, as Abraham sacrificing his son Isaac, Judith killing Holofernes, David fighting with Goliath – may leave those and please an ill-pleased [pleased with evil] eye with wanton shows of better hidden matters. But what, shall the abuse of a thing make the right use odious? Nay truly, though I yield that Poesy may not only be abused, but that being abused (by the reason of his sweet charming force) it can do more hurt than any other army of words, yet shall it be so far from concluding that the abuse should give reproach to the abused, that contrariwise it is a good reason, that whatsoever, being abused, doth most harm, being rightly used (and upon the right use each thing receives his title), doth most good.

Do we not see the skill of Physic (the best rampire [defence] to our often-assaulted bodies), being abused, teach poison, the most violent destroyer? Doth not knowledge of Law, whose end is to even and right all things, being abused, grow the crooked fosterer of horrible injuries? Doth not (to go to the highest) God's word abused breed heresy, and His name abused become blasphemy? Truly a needle cannot do much hurt, and as truly (with leave of ladies be it spoken) it cannot do much good. With a sword thou mayest kill thy father, and with a sword thou mayest defend thy prince and country. So that, as in their calling poets the father of lies they say nothing, so in this their argument of abuse they prove the commendation.

They allege herewith that before poets began to be in price [valued] our nation had set their hearts' delight upon action, and not imagination, rather doing things worthy to be written, than writing things fit to be done. What that beforetime was, I think scarcely Sphinx can tell, since no memory is so ancient that hath the precedence of Poetry. And certain it is that, in our plainest homeliness, yet never was the Albion nation without Poetry. Marry, this argument, though it be levelled against Poetry, yet is it indeed a chainshot against all learning, or bookishness, as they commonly term it. Of such a mind were certain Goths, of whom it is written that, having in the spoil of a famous city [Athens] taken a fair library, one hangman [base villain] (belike fit to execute the fruits of their wits who had murdered a great number of bodies) would have set fire on it. "No," said another gravely, "take heed what you do, for while they are busy about these toys, we shall with more leisure conquer their countries".

This indeed is the ordinary doctrine of ignorance, and many words sometimes I have heard spent in it; but because this reason is generally against all learning, as well as Poetry, or rather, all learning but Poetry; because it were too large a digression to handle it, or at least too superfluous (since it is manifest that all government of action is to be gotten by knowledge, and knowledge best by gathering many knowledges, which is reading), I only, with Horace, to him that is of that opinion, *jubeo stultum esse libenter* [bid him be a fool if he wishes]; for as for Poetry itself, it is the freest from this objection.

For Poetry is the companion of the camps. I dare undertake, Orlando Furioso, or honest King Arthur, will never displease a soldier; but the quiddity of *ens* and *prima materia* will hardly agree with a corslet [body armour].* And therefore, as I said in the beginning, even Turks and Tartars are delighted with poets. Homer, a Greek, flourished before Greece flourished. And if to a slight conjecture a conjecture may be opposed, truly it may seem, that as by him their learned men took almost their first motions of courage. Only Alexander's army may serve, who by Plutarch is accounted of such virtue that Fortune was not his guide but his footstool; whose acts speak for him, though [even if] Plutarch did not – indeed the phoenix of warlike princes. This Alexander left his schoolmaster, living Aristotle, behind him, but took dead Homer with him. He put the philosopher Callisthenes to death for his seeming philosophical, indeed mutinous, stubbornness, but the chief thing he ever was heard to wish for was that Homer had been alive. He well found he received more bravery of mind by the pattern of Achilles than by hearing the definition of fortitude. And therefore, if Cato mislike Fulvius for carrying Ennius with him to the field, it may be answered that, if Cato misliked it, the noble Fulvius liked it, or else he had not done it:* for it was not the excellent Cato Uticensis (whose authority I would much more have reverenced) but it was the former, in truth a bitter punisher of faults, but else a man that had never well sacrificed to the graces. He misliked and cried out against all Greek learning and yet, being four score years old, began to learn it, belike fearing that Pluto understood not Latin. Indeed, the Roman laws allowed no person to be carried to the wars but he that was in the soldiers' roll, and therefore, though Cato misliked his unmustered person [i.e. Ennius], he misliked not his work. And if he had, Scipio Nasica, judged by common consent the best Roman, loved him. Both the other Scipio brothers, who had by their virtues [military victories in those places] no less surnames than of Asia and Afric, so loved him that they caused his body to be buried in their sepulchre. So as Cato's authority being but against his person, and that answered with so far greater than himself, is herein of no validity.

But now indeed my burden is great, that Plato's name is laid upon me, whom I must confess, of all philosophers I have ever esteemed most worthy of reverence, and with good reason – since of all philosophers he is the most poetical. Yet if he will defile the fountain out of which his flowing streams have proceeded, let us boldly examine with what reasons he did it. First, truly a man might maliciously object Plato, being a philosopher, was a natural enemy of poets. For indeed, after the philosophers had picked out of the sweet mysteries of Poetry the right discerning true points of knowledge, they forthwith – putting it in method, and making a school-art of that which the poets did only teach by a divine delightfulness, beginning to spurn at their guides, like ungrateful prentices – were not content to set up shops for themselves, but sought by all means to discredit their masters; which by the force of delight being barred them, the less they could overthrow them, the more they hated them. For indeed, they found for Homer seven cities strave who should have him for their citizen; where many cities banished philosophers as not fit members to live among them. For only repeating certain of Euripides' verses, many Athenians had their lives saved of the Syracusans, when the Athenians themselves thought many philosophers unworthy to live. Certain poets, as Simonides and Pindar, had so prevailed with Hiero the First that of a tyrant they made him a just king; where Plato could do so little with Dionysius, that he himself of a philosopher was made a slave.* But who should do thus [i.e. "maliciously object"], I confess, should requite the objections made against poets with like cavillations against philosophers; as likewise one should do that should bid one read *Phaedrus* or *Symposium* in Plato, or the discourse of love in Plutarch, and see whether any poet do authorize abominable filthiness [probably homosexuality], as they do. Again, a man might ask out of what commonwealth Plato did banish them. In sooth, thence where he himself alloweth community of women

134

[*The Republic*, V]. So as belike this banishment grew not for effemi-
nate wantonness, since little should poetical sonnets be hurtful
when a man might have what woman he listed. But I honour
philosophical instructions, and bless the wits which bred them:
so as they be not abused, which is likewise stretched to Poetry.

St. Paul himself (who yet, for the credit of poets, allegeth
[quotes] twice two poets, and one of them by the name of a
prophet),* sets a watchword [warning; Colossians 2: 8] upon
Philosophy – indeed upon the abuse. So doth Plato upon the
abuse, not upon Poetry. Plato found fault that the poets of his
time filled the world with wrong opinions of the gods, making
light tales of that unspotted essence, and therefore would not
have the youth depraved with such opinions. Herein may much
be said; let this suffice: the poets did not induce [introduce] such
opinions, but did imitate those opinions already induced. For all
the Greek stories can well testify that the very religion of that
time stood upon many and many-fashioned gods, not taught so
by poets, but followed according to their nature of imitation.
Who list may read in Plutarch the discourses of Isis and Osiris,
of the cause why oracles ceased, of the divine providence, and
see whether the theology of that nation stood not upon such
dreams, which the poets indeed superstitiously observed and
truly (since they had not the light of Christ) did much better in
it than the philosophers who, shaking off superstition, brought
in atheism. Plato therefore (whose authority I had much rather
justly construe than unjustly resist) meant not in general of poets,
in those words of which Julius Scaliger saith, *Qua authoritate bar-
bari quidam atque hispidi abuti velint ad poetas e republica exigendos;**
but only meant to drive out those wrong opinions of the Deity
(whereof now, without further law, Christianity hath taken away
all the hurtful belief), perchance (as he thought) nourished by
the then esteemed poets. And a man need go no further than to
Plato himself to know his meaning: who, in his dialogue called
Ion, giveth high and rightly divine commendation to Poetry. So
as Plato, banishing the abuse, not the thing – not banishing it,
but giving due honour unto it – shall be our patron and not our
adversary. For indeed I had much rather (since truly I may do it)
show their mistaking of Plato (under whose lion's skin they would

make an ass-like braying against Poesy) than go about to over-throw his authority; whom, the wiser a man is, the more just cause he shall find to have in admiration; especially since he attributeth unto Poesy more than myself do, namely, to be a very inspiring of a divine force, far above man's wit, as in the fore-named dialogue is apparent.

Of the other side, who would show the honours ["which" understood] have been by the best sort of judgements granted them, a whole sea of examples would present themselves: Alexanders, Caesars, Scipios, all favourers of poets; Laelius, called the Roman Socrates, himself a poet, so as part of *Heautontimorumenos* in Terence was supposed to be made by him; and even the Greek Socrates, whom Apollo confirmed to be the only wise man [see *Astrophil and Stella*, 25], is said to have spent part of his old time in putting Aesop's fables into verses. And therefore, full evil should it become his scholar Plato to put such words in his master's mouth against poets. But what needs more? Aristotle writes the Art of Poesy: and why, if it should not be written? Plutarch teacheth the use to be gathered of them, and how, if they should not be read? And who reads Plutarch's either history or philosophy, shall find he trimmeth both their garments with guards [orna-mental borders] of Poesy. But I list not to defend Poesy with the help of her underling Historiography. Let it suffice to have showed that it is a fit soil for praise to dwell upon; and what dispraise may set upon it, is either easily overcome, or trans-formed into just commendation.

So that, since the excellencies of it may be so easily and so justly confirmed, and the low-creeping objections so soon trod-den down: it not being an art of lies, but of true doctrine; not of effeminateness, but of notable stirring of courage; not of abusing man's wit, but of strengthening man's wit; not banished, but honoured by Plato; let us rather plant more laurels for to engar-land our poets' heads (which honour of being laureate, as besides them only triumphant captains wear, is a sufficient authority to show the price they ought to be held in) than suffer the ill-savoured breath of such wrong-speakers once to blow upon the clear springs of Poesy.

But since I have run so long a career [course] in this matter, methinks, before I give my pen a full stop, it shall be but a little more lost time to enquire why England, the mother of excellent minds, should be grown so hard a stepmother to poets, who certainly in wit ought to pass all others, since all only proceeds from their wit, being indeed makers of themselves, not takers of others. How can I but exclaim, *Musa, mihi causas memora, quo numine laeso?**

Sweet Poesy, that hath anciently had kings, emperors, senators, great captains, such as, besides a thousand others, David, Adrian, Sophocles, Germanicus, not only to favour poets, but to be poets; and of our nearer times can present for her patrons a Robert, king of Sicily, the great King Francis of France, King James of Scotland;* such cardinals as Bembus and Bibbiena; such famous preachers and teachers as Beza and Melanchthon; so learned philosophers as Fracastorius and Scaliger; so great orators as Pontanus and Muretus; so piercing wits as George Buchanan; so grave counsellors as, besides many, but before all, that Hospital of France,* than whom (I think) that realm never brought forth a more accomplished judgement, more firmly builded upon virtue – I say these, with numbers of others, not only to read others' poesies, but to poetise for others' reading – that Poesy, thus embraced in all other places, should only find in our time a hard welcome in England, I think the very earth lamenteth it, and therefore decks our soil with fewer laurels than it was accustomed. For heretofore poets have in England also flourished and, which is to be noted, even in those times when the trumpet of Mars did sound loudest. And now that an overfaint quietness should seem to strew the house for poets, they are almost in as good reputation as the mountebanks at Venice. Truly even that, as of the one side it giveth great praise to Poesy, which like Venus – but to better purpose – hath rather be troubled in the net with Mars than enjoy the homely quiet of Vulcan; so serves it for a piece of a reason why they are less grateful [pleasing] to idle England, which now can scarce endure the pain of a pen. Upon this necessarily followeth, that base men with servile wits undertake it, who think it enough if they can be rewarded of the printer. And so as Epaminondas* is said, with the honour of his virtue

137

to have made an office, by his exercising it, which before was contemptible, to become highly respected, so these men, no more but setting their names to it, by their own disgracefulness disgrace the most graceful Poesy. For now, as if all the Muses were got with child to bring forth bastard poets, without any commission they do pass over the banks of Helicon, till they make the readers more weary than post-horses; while in the meantime they, *Queis meliore luto finxit praecordia Titan,** are better content to suppress the outflowings of their wit than, by publishing them, to be accounted knights of the same order.

But I that, before ever I durst aspire unto the dignity, am admitted into the company of the paper-blurrers, do find the very true cause of our wanting estimation is want of desert, taking upon us to be poets in despite of Pallas [i.e. scorning wisdom]. Now wherein we want desert were a thankworthy labour to express; but if I knew, I should have mended myself. But I, as I never desired the title, so have I neglected the means to come by it. Only, overmastered by some thoughts, I yielded an inky tribute unto them. Marry, they that delight in Poesy itself should seek to know what they do, and how they do; and especially look themselves in an unflattering glass of reason, if they be inclinable unto it. For Poesy must not be drawn by the ears; it must be gently led, or rather it must lead; which was partly the cause that made the ancient learned affirm it was a divine gift, and no human skill – since all other knowledges lie ready for any that have strength of wit; a poet no industry can make, if his own genius be not carried unto it; and therefore is it an old proverb, *orator fit, poeta nascitur* [an orator is made; a poet is born]. Yet confess I always that as the fertilest ground must be manured [cultivated], so must the highest-flying wit have a Daedalus* to guide him. That Daedalus, they say, both in this and in other, hath three wings to bear itself up into the air of due commendation: that is, Art, Imitation [following earlier models], and Exercise. But these, neither artificial rules nor imitative patterns, we much cumber ourselves withal. Exercise indeed we do, but that very fore-backwardly: for where we should exercise to know, we exercise as having known; and so is our brain delivered of much matter which never was begotten by knowledge. For there being two principal parts – matter to be expressed by words and words to express the matter – in neither we use Art or Imitation rightly. Our matter is *quodlibet* [whatever you like] indeed, though wrongly performing Ovid's verse, *Quicquid conabor dicere, versus erit:** never marshalling it into any assured rank, that almost the readers cannot tell where to find themselves.

Chaucer undoubtedly did excellently in his *Troilus and Criseyde*; of whom truly I know not whether to marvel more, either that he in that misty time could see so clearly, or that we in this clear age walk so stumblingly after him. Yet had he great wants, fit to be forgiven in so reverent an antiquity. I account the *Mirror of Magistrates* meetly furnished of beautiful parts, and in the Earl of Surrey's lyrics many things tasting of noble birth, and worthy of a noble mind. The *Shepherd's Calendar* hath much poetry in his eclogues, indeed worthy the reading, if I be not deceived. That same framing of his style to an old rustic language I dare not allow [commend], since neither Theocritus in Greek, Virgil in Latin, nor Sannazzaro in Italian did affect it.* Besides these, I do not remember to have seen but few (to speak boldly) printed, that have poetical sinews in them. For proof whereof, let but most of the verses be put in prose, and then ask the meaning, and it will be found that one verse did but beget another, without ordering at the first what should be at the last; which becomes a confused mass of words, with a tingling sound of rhyme, barely accompanied with reason.

Our Tragedies and Comedies (not without cause cried out against), observing rules neither of honest civility nor of skilful Poetry, excepting *Gorboduc** (again, I say, of those that I have seen), which notwithstanding, as it is full of stately speeches and well-sounding phrases, climbing to the height of Seneca's style, and as full of notable morality, which it doth most delightfully teach, and so obtain the very end of Poesy, yet in truth it is very defectious in the circumstances [formal particulars], which grieves me, because it might not remain as an exact model of all tragedies. For it is faulty both in place and time, the two necessary companions of all corporal actions. For where the stage should always represent but one place, and the uttermost time presupposed in it should be, both by Aristotle's precept and common

reason, but one day, there is both many days and places, inarti-
ficially [unskilfully] imagined.

But if it be so in *Gorboduc*, how much more in all the rest? where
you shall have Asia of the one side, and Afric of the other, and
so many other under-kingdoms, that the player, when he comes
in, must ever begin telling where he is, or else the tale will not
be conceived. Now you shall have three ladies walk to gather
flowers and then we must believe the stage to be a garden. By
and by we hear news of shipwreck in the same place and then
we are to blame if we accept it not for a rock. Upon the back of
that comes out a hideous monster with fire and smoke and then
the miserable beholders are bound to take it for a cave. While in
the meantime two armies fly in, represented with four swords
and bucklers, and then what hard heart will not receive it for a
pitched field?

Now of time they are much more liberal, for ordinary it is that
two young princes fall in love. After many traverses [passages/
obstacles], she is got with child, delivered of a fair boy, he is lost,
groweth a man, falls in love, and is ready to get another child,
and all this in two hours' space – which how absurd it is in sense,
even sense may imagine, and Art hath taught, and all ancient
examples justified, and at this day the ordinary players in Italy
will not err in. Yet will some bring in an example of *Eunuchus* in
Terence, that containeth matter of two days, yet far short of
twenty years. True it is, and so was it to be played in two days,
and so fitted to the time it set forth. And though Plautus hath in
one place [*Captives*] done amiss, let us hit with him, and not miss
with him. But they will say: how then shall we set forth a story
which contains both many places and many times? And do they
not know that a tragedy is tied to the laws of Poesy, and not of
History; not bound to follow the story, but having liberty either
to feign a quite new matter or to frame the history to the most
tragical conveniency? Again, many things may be told which
cannot be showed, if they know the difference betwixt reporting
and representing. As, for example, I may speak (though I am
here) of Peru, and in speech digress from that to the description
of Calicut; but in action I cannot represent it without Pacolet's
horse.* And so was the manner the ancients took, by some *nuncius*

[messenger] to recount things done in former time or other place.

Lastly, if they will represent an history, they must not (as Horace saith) begin *ab ovo* [from the egg/beginning], but they must come to the principal point of that one action which they will represent. By example this will be best expressed. I have a story of young Polydorus [from Euripides' *Hecuba*], delivered for safety's sake with great riches, by his father Priam to Polymnestor, King of Thrace, in the Trojan war time. He, after some years, hearing the overthrow of Priam, for to make the treasure his own, murdereth the child. The body of the child is taken up by Hecuba. She, the same day, findeth a sleight to be revenged most cruelly of the tyrant. Where now would one of our tragedy writers begin, but with the delivery [birth] of the child? Then should he sail over into Thrace, and so spend I know not how many years, and travel numbers of places. But where doth Euripides? Even with the finding of the body, leaving the rest to be told by the spirit of Polydorus. This needs no further to be enlarged; the dullest wit may conceive it.

But besides these gross absurdities, how all their [modern writers'] plays be neither right tragedies nor right comedies, mingling kings and clowns, not because the matter so carrieth it, but thrust in the clown by head and shoulders to play a part in majestical matters, with neither decency nor discretion, so as neither the admiration and commiseration [traditionally proper to tragedy], nor the right sportfulness [of comedy], is by their mongrel tragi-comedy obtained. I know Apuleius did somewhat so [in *The Golden Ass*], but that is a thing recounted with space of time, not represented in one moment; and I know the ancients have one or two examples of tragi-comedies, as Plautus hath *Amphitrio*. But if we mark them well, we shall find that they never, or very daintily, match hornpipes and funerals. So falleth it out that, having indeed no right comedy, in that comical part of our tragedy, we have nothing but scurrility, unworthy of any chaste ears, or some extreme show of doltishness, indeed fit to lift up a loud laughter, and nothing else; where the whole trace [extent/treatment] of a comedy should be full of delight, as the tragedy should be still maintained in a well-raised admiration.

But our comedians think there is no delight without laughter;

which is very wrong, for though laughter may come with delight, yet cometh it not of delight, as though delight should be the cause of laughter; but well may one thing breed both together. Nay, rather in themselves they have, as it were, a kind of contrariety – for delight we scarcely do but in things that have a conveniency to ourselves or to the general nature; laughter almost ever cometh of things most disproportioned to ourselves and nature. Delight hath a joy in it, either permanent or present. Laughter hath only a scornful tickling. For example, we are ravished with delight to see a fair woman, and yet are far from being moved to laughter. We laugh at deformed creatures, wherein certainly we cannot delight. We delight in good chances, we laugh at mischances; we delight to hear the happiness of friends or country, at which he were worthy to be laughed at that would laugh. We shall, contrarily, laugh sometimes to find a matter quite mistaken and go down the hill against the bias, in the mouth of some such men as for the respect of them one shall be heartily sorry, yet he cannot choose but laugh; and so is rather pained than delighted with laughter. Yet deny I not but that they may go well together: for as in Alexander's picture well set out we delight without laughter, and in twenty mad antics we laugh without delight; so in Hercules, painted with his great beard and furious countenance, in woman's attire, spinning at Omphale's commandment, it breeds both delight and laughter. For the representing of so strange a power in love procures delight; and the scornfulness of the action stirreth laughter.

But I speak to this purpose, that all the end of the comical part be not upon such scornful matters as stir laughter only, but mixed with it that delightful teaching which is the end of Poesy. And the great fault even in that point of laughter, and forbidden plainly by Aristotle, is that they stir laughter in sinful things, which are rather execrable than ridiculous; or in miserable, which are rather to be pitied than scorned. For what is it to make folks gape at a wretched beggar or a beggarly clown [peasant]; or, against law of hospitality, to jest at strangers because they speak not English so well as we do? What do we learn? since it is certain

Nil habet infelix paupertas durius in se,
Quam quod ridiculos homines facit.*

But rather a busy loving courtier; a heartless threatening Thraso; a self-wise-seeming schoolmaster; an awry-transformed [affected] traveller – these if we saw walk in stage names, which we play naturally, therein were delightful laughter and teaching delight-fulness; as in the other, the tragedies of Buchanan do justly bring forth a divine admiration. But I have lavished out too many words of this play matter. I do it because, as they are excelling parts of Poesy, so is there none so much used in England, and none can be more pitifully abused; which, like an unmannerly daughter showing a bad education, causeth her mother Poesy's honesty to be called in question.

Other sorts of Poetry almost have we none, but that lyrical kind of songs and sonnets: which, Lord, if He gave us so good minds, how well it might be employed, and with how heavenly fruits, both private and public, in singing the praises of the immortal beauty, the immortal goodness of that God who giveth us hands to write and wits to conceive; of which we might well want words, but never matter; of which we could turn our eyes to nothing, but we should ever have new-budding occasions. But truly many of such writings as come under the banner of unresistible love, if I were a mistress, would never persuade me they were in love. So coldly they apply fiery speeches, as men that had rather read lovers' writings (and so caught up certain swelling phrases which hang together, like a man which once told me the wind was at north-west and by south, because he would be sure to name winds enough), than that in truth they feel those passions, which easily – as I think – may be betrayed by that same forcibleness or *energia* (as the Greeks call it) of the writer. But let this be a sufficient though short note, that we miss the right use of the material point of Poesy.

Now, for the outside of it, which is words, or (as I may term it) diction [choice of words], it is even well worse. So is that honey-flowing matron eloquence apparelled, or rather disguised, in a courtesan-like painted affectation: one time with so far-fetched words that may seem monsters, but must seem strangers, to any poor Englishman; another time with coursing of a letter [earnest alliteration], as if they were bound to follow the method of a dictionary; another time with figures and flowers [rhetorical figures; see *Astrophil and Stella*, 15 & Ninth Song] extremely winter-starved. But I would this fault were only peculiar to versifiers, and had not as large possession among prose-printers, and (which is to be marvelled) among many scholars, and (which is to be pitied) among some preachers. Truly I could wish, if at least I might be so bold to wish in a thing beyond the reach of my capacity, the diligent imitators of Tully and Demosthenes (most worthy to be imitated) did not so much keep Nizolian paper-books of their figures and phrases,* as by attentive translation [transformation/legal transfer] (as it were) devour them whole, and make them wholly theirs. For now they cast sugar and spice upon every dish that is served to the table, like those Indians not content to wear earrings at the fit and natural place of the ears, but they will thrust jewels through their nose and lips, because they will be sure to be fine.

Tully, when he was to drive out Catiline as it were with a thunderbolt of eloquence, often used the figure of repetition: *Vivit. Vivit? Imo vero etiam in senatum venit,** &c. Indeed, inflamed with a well-grounded rage, he would have his words (as it were) double out of his mouth, and so do that artificially which we see men do in choler naturally. And we, having noted the grace of those words, hale them in sometimes to a familiar epistle, when it were too much collar to be choleric. How well store of *similiter cadences* [similar patterned endings of sentences] doth sound with the gravity of the pulpit, I would but invoke Demosthenes' soul to tell, who with a rare daintiness useth them. Truly they have made me think of the sophister [logician] that with too much subtlety would prove two eggs three and, though he might be counted a sophister, had none for his labour. So these men bringing in such a kind of eloquence, well may they obtain an opinion of seeming fineness, but persuade few – which should be the end of their fineness.

Now for similitudes [similes; see *Astrophil and Stella*, 3] in certain printed discourses, I think all herbarists, all stories of beasts, fowls, and fishes are rifled up, that they come in multitudes to wait upon any of our conceits; which certainly is as absurd a surfeit to the ears as is possible: for the force of a similitude not being to prove anything to a contrary disputer, but only to explain to a willing hearer; when that is done, the rest is a most tedious prattling, rather overswaying the memory from the purpose whereto they were applied than any whit informing the judgement, already either satisfied or by similitudes not to be satisfied. For my part, I do not doubt, when Antonius and Crassus, the great forefather of Cicero in eloquence, the one (as Cicero testifieth of them) pretended not to know art, the other not to set by it, because with a plain sensibleness they might win credit of popular ears; which credit is the nearest step to persuasion; which persuasion is the chief mark of Oratory – I do not doubt (I say) but that they used these knacks [tricks or habits of speech] very sparingly; which, who doth generally use, any man may see doth dance to his own music, and so be noted by the audience more careful to speak curiously [elaborately] than truly.

Undoubtedly (at least to my opinion undoubtedly) I have found in divers small-learned courtiers a more sound style than in some professors of learning; of which I can guess no other cause, but that the courtier – following that which he findeth fittest to nature – therein (though he know it not) doth according to art, though not by art; where the other, using art to show art, and not to hide art (as in these cases he should do), flieth from nature and indeed abuseth art.

But what? methinks I deserve to be pounded for straying from Poetry to Oratory; but both have such an affinity in this wordish consideration [i.e. diction] that I think this digression will make my meaning receive the fuller understanding – which is not to take upon me to teach poets how they should do, but only (finding myself sick among the rest) to show some one or two spots of the common infection grown among the most part of writers; that, acknowledging ourselves somewhat awry, we may bend to the right use both of matter and manner; whereunto our language giveth us great occasion, being indeed capable of any excellent exercising of it. I know some will say it is a mingled language [derived from more than one source]. And why not so much the better, taking the best of both the other?* Another will say it wanteth grammar. Nay truly, it hath that praise that it wants not grammar – for grammar it might have, but it needs it not; being so easy in itself, and so void of those cumbersome differences of

145

cases, genders, moods, and tenses, which I think was a piece of the Tower of Babylon's [associated with Babel] curse, that a man should be put to school to learn his mother-tongue. But for the uttering sweetly and properly the conceits of the mind, which is the end of speech, that hath it equally with any other tongue in the world; and is particularly happy in compositions of two or three words together [compound words], near the Greek, far beyond the Latin; which is one of the greatest beauties can be in a language.

Now of versifying there are two sorts, the one ancient, the other modern: the ancient marked the quantity [assigned length of vowels] of each syllable, and according to that framed his verse; the modern observing only number [metred syllables] (with some regard of the accent), the chief life of it standeth in that like sounding of the words which we call rhyme. Whether [which] of these be the most excellent would bear many speeches: the ancient (no doubt) more fit for music, both words and time observing quantity, and more fit lively to express divers passions, by the low or lofty sound of the well-weighed syllable. The latter likewise, with his rhyme, striketh a certain music to the ear; and, in fine, since it doth delight, though by another way, it obtains the same purpose – there being in either sweetness, and wanting in neither majesty. Truly the English, before any other vulgar language I know, is fit for both sorts: for, for the ancient, the Italian is so full of vowels that it must ever be cumbered with elisions [contractions of adjoining vowels]; the Dutch [i.e. Deutsch, German] so, of the other side, with consonants, that they cannot yield the sweet sliding fit for a verse; the French in his whole language hath not one word that hath his accent in the last syllable, saving two, called *antepenultima*; and little more hath the Spanish, and therefore very gracelessly may they use dactyls. The English is subject to none of these defects.

Now for the rhyme [modern accentual verse], though we do not observe quantity, yet we observe the accent very precisely, which other languages either cannot do, or will not do so absolutely. That *caesura*, or breathing place in the midst of the verse, neither Italian nor Spanish have, the French and we never almost fail of. Lastly, even the very rhyme itself: the Italian cannot put it in the last syllable, by the French named the masculine rhyme, but still in the next to last, which the French call the female, or the next before that, which the Italians term *sdrucciola*. The example of the former is *buono : suono*, of the *sdrucciola, femina : semina*. The French, of the other side, hath both the male, as *bon : son*, and the female, as *plaise : taise*, but the *sdrucciola* he hath not – where the English hath all three, as *due : true, father : rather, motion : potion*; with much more which might be said, but that I find already the triflingness of this discourse is much too much enlarged.

So that since the ever-praiseworthy Poesy is full of virtue-breeding delightfulness, and void of no gift that ought to be in the noble name of learning; since the blames laid against it are either false or feeble; since the cause why it is not esteemed in England is the fault of poet-apes, not poets; since, lastly, our tongue is most fit to honour Poesy and to be honoured by Poesy; I conjure you all that have had the evil luck to read this ink-wasting toy of mine, even in the name of the Nine Muses, no more to scorn the sacred mysteries of Poesy, no more to laugh at the name of poets as though they were next inheritors to fools, no more to jest at the reverent title of a rhymer; but to believe, with Aristotle, that they were the ancient treasurers of the Grecians' divinity; to believe, with Bembus, that they were the first bringers-in of all civility; to believe, with Scaliger, that no philosopher's precepts can sooner make you an honest man than the reading of Virgil; to believe, with Clauserus, the translator of Cornutus, that it pleased the heavenly Deity, by Hesiod and Homer, under the veil of fables, to give us all knowledge, Logic, Rhetoric, Philosophy natural and moral, and *quid non?* [what not]; to believe, with me, that there are many mysteries contained in Poetry, which of purpose were written darkly, lest by prophane wits it should be abused; to believe, with Landino, that they are so beloved of the gods that whatsoever they write proceeds of a divine fury; lastly, to believe themselves, when they tell you they will make you immortal by their verses.

Thus doing, your name shall flourish in the printers' shops; thus doing, you shall be of kin to many a poetical preface; thus doing, you shall be most fair, most rich, most wise, most all; you shall dwell upon superlatives. Thus doing, though you be *libertino patre natus* [son of a freedman], you shall suddenly grow *Herculea proles* [a child of Hercules], *Si quid mea carmina possunt*.* Thus doing, your soul shall be placed with Dante's Beatrix, or Virgil's Anchises. But if (fie of such a but) you be born so near the dull-making cataract of Nilus that you cannot hear the planet-like music of Poetry; if you have so earth-creeping a mind that it cannot lift itself up to look to the sky of Poetry, or rather, by a certain rustical disdain, will become such a mome [blockhead] as to be a Momus of Poetry; then, though I will not wish unto you the ass's ears of Midas, nor to be driven by a poet's verses (as Bubonax was) to hang himself,* nor to be rhymed to death, as is said to be done in Ireland; yet thus much curse I must send you, in the behalf of all poets, that while you live, you live in love, and never get favour for lacking skill of a sonnet, and when you die, your memory die from the earth for want of an epitaph.

Miscellaneous Poems

The lad Philisides
Lay by a river's side,
In flow'ry field a gladder eye to please:[†]
His pipe was at his foot,
His lambs were him beside,
A widow turtle[†] near on bared root
Sat wailing without boot.[†]
Each thing both sweet and sad
Did draw his boiling brain
To think, and think with pain
Of Mira's beams eclips'd by absence bad.
And thus, with eyes made dim
With tears, he said, or sorrow said for him:

"O earth, once answer give,
So may thy stately grace
By north or south still rich adorned live:
So Mira long may be
On thy then blessed face,
Whose foot doth set a heav'n on cursed thee;
I ask, now answer me.
If th'author of thy bliss,
Phoebus, that shepherd high,
Do turn from thee his eye,
Doth not thyself, when he long absent is,
Like rogue,[†] all ragged go,
And pine away with daily wasting woe?

"Tell me you wanton brook,
So may your sliding race
Shun loathed-loving banks with cunning crook:[†]
So in you ever new
Mira may look her face,

And make you fair with shadow of her hue:
So when to pay your due
To mother sea you come,
She chide you not for stay,
Nor beat you for your play, –
Tell me, if your diverted springs become
Absented quite from you,
Are you not dried? Can you yourselves renew?

"Tell me you flowers fair,
Cowslip and columbine,
So may your make,† this wholesome springtime air,
With you embraced lie,
And lately thence untwine:
But with dew drops engender children high:
So may you never die,
But pull'd by Mira's hand,
Dress bosom hers, or head,
Or scatter on her bed, –
Tell me, if husband springtime leave your land,
When he from you is sent,
Wither not you, languish'd with discontent?

"Tell me, my silly pipe,
So may thee still betide,
A cleanly cloth thy moistness for to wipe:
So may the cherries red
Of Mira's lips divide
Their sugared selves to kiss thy happy head:
So may her ears be led,
Her ears where music lives,
To hear and not despise
Thy liribliring† cries, –
Tell, if that breath, which thee thy sounding gives,
Be absent far from thee,
Absent alone canst thou then piping be?

"Tell me my lamb of gold,
So may'st thou long abide
The day well fed, the night in faithful fold:
So grow thy wool of note,
In time that, richly dy'd,
It may be part of Mira's petticoat, –
Tell me, if wolves the throat
Have caught of thy dear dam,
Or she from thee be stay'd,
Or thou from her be stray'd,
Canst thou, poor lamb, become another's lamb?
Or rather, till thou die,
Still for thy dam with baa-waymenting[†] cry?

"Tell me, O turtle true,
So may no fortune breed
To make thee nor thy better-loved rue:
So may thy blessings swarm
That Mira may thee feed
With hand and mouth, with lap and breast keep warm, –
Tell me if greedy arm
Do fondly[†] take away
With traitor lime[†] the one,
The other left alone, –
Tell me, poor wretch, parted from wretched prey,[†]
Disdain not you the green,
Wailing till death, shun you not to be seen?

"Earth, brook, flow'rs, pipe, lamb, dove,
Say all, and I with them,
'Absence is death, or worse, to them that love.'
So I unlucky lad
Whom hills from her do hem,[†]
What fits me now but tears, and sighings sad?
O fortune too too bad,
I rather would my sheep
Th'ad'st killed with a stroke,
Burnt cabin, lost my cloak,

151

Than want one hour those eyes which my joys keep.
Oh, what doth wailing win?
Speech without end were better not begin.

"My song climb thou the wind
Which Holland sweet now gently sendeth in,
That on his wings the level[†] thou may'st find
To hit, but kissing hit,[†]
Her ears the weights[†] of wit.
If thou know not for whom thy master dies,
These marks shall make thee wise:
She is the herdess fair that shines in dark
And gives her kids no food, but willow's bark."[†]

This said, at length he ended
His oft sigh-broken ditty,
Then rase, but rase on legs with faintness bended,
With skin in sorrow dyed,
With face the plot of pity,
With thoughts which thoughts their own tormentors tried.
He rase, and straight espied
His ram, who to recover
The ewe another loved,
With him proud battle proved.
He envied such a death in sight of lover,
And always westward eyeing,
More envied Phoebus for his western flying.

to please able to please; *turtle* turtle dove (proverbially constant lover); *boot* remedy; *rogue* vagabond; *crook* turning aside; *make* mate; *silly* innocent; *liribliring* imitation of a pipe's sound; *baa-waymenting* lamenting by crying "baa"; *fondly* madly; *lime* bird lime, used in trapping; *prey* captured mate; *hem* shut out; *level* aim; *kissing hit* touch lightly; *weights* scales; *willow's bark* sorrow's food; *plot* map; *rase* rose

As I my little flock on Ister bank[†]
(A little flock; but well my pipe they couth[†])
Did piping lead, the sun already sank
Beyond our world, and ere I gatt my booth,[†]
Each thing with mantle black the night did scothe;[†]
   Saving the glow-worm, which would courteous be
   Of that small light oft watching shepherds see.

The welkin[†] had full niggardly enclosed
In coffer of dim clowds his silver groats,
Ycleped[†] stars; each thing to rest disposed;
The caves were full, the mountains void of goats:
The birds' eyes clos'd, closed their chirping notes.
   As for the nightingale, woodmusic's king,
   It August was, he deign'd not then to sing.

Amid my sheep, though I saw nought to fear,
Yet (for I nothing saw) I feared sore;
Then found I which thing is a charge to bear,
As for my sheep I dreaded mickle more
Than ever for myself since I was bore:
   I sat me down, for see to go ne could,
   And sang unto my sheep lest stray they should.

The song I sang old Languet had me taught,
Languet, the shepherd best swift Ister knew,
For clerkly rede,[†] and hating what is naught,
For faithful heart, clean hands, and mouth as true:
With his sweet skill my skilless youth he drew
   To have a feeling taste of him that sits
   Beyond the heaven, far more beyond your wits.

He said, the music best thilk powers pleas'd
Was jump[†] concord between our wit and will:
Where highest notes to godliness are rais'd,
And lowest sink not down to jot of ill:

With old true tales he wont mine ears to fill,
    How shepherds did of yore, how now they thrive,
    Spoiling their flock, or while 'twixt them they strive.

He liked me, but pitied lustful youth:
His good strong staff my slipp'ry years upbore:
He still hop'd well, because I loved truth;
Till forc'd to part, with heart and eyes e'en sore,
To worthy Coriden[†] he gave me o'er;
    But thus in oak's true shade recounted he
    Which now in night's deep shade sheep heard of me.

Such manner time there was (what time I n'ot[†])
When all this earth, this dam or mould of ours,
Was only won'd[†] with such as beasts begot:
Unknown as then were they that builded towers:
The cattle wild, or tame, in nature's bowers
    Might freely roam, or rest, as seemed them:
    Man was not man their dwellings in to hem.

The beasts had sure some beastly policy:
For nothing can endure where order n'is.[†]
For once the lion by the lamb did lie;
The fearful hind the leopard did kiss:
Hurtless was tiger's paw and serpent's hiss.[†]
    This think I well, the beasts with courage clad
    Like senators a harmless empire had.

At which, whether the others did repine,
(For envy harb'reth most in feeblest hearts)
Or that they all to changing did encline,
(As even in beasts their dams leave changing parts)
The multitude to Jove a suit imparts,
    With neighing, blaying,[†] braying, and barking,
    Roaring and howling for to have a king.

A king, in language theirs they said they would
(For then their language was a perfect speech)
The birds likewise with chirps, and pewing[†] could,
Cackling and chatt'ring, that of Jove beseech.
Only the owl still warn'd them not to seech[†]
 So hastily that which they would repent:
 But saw they would, and he to deserts went.

Jove wisely said (for wisdom wisely says)
"O beasts, take heed what you of me desire.
Rulers will think all things made them to please,
And soon forget the swink[†] due to their hire:
But since you will, part of my heav'nly fire
 I will you lend; the rest yourselves must give,
 That it both seen and felt may with you live."

Full glad they were and took the naked sprite,
Which straight the earth yclothed in his clay:
The lion, heart; the ounce[†] gave active might;
The horse, good shape; the sparrow, lust to play;
Nightingale, voice, enticing songs to say.
 Elephant gave a perfect memory:
 And parrot, ready tongue, that to apply.

The fox gave craft; the dog gave flattery;
Ass patience; the mole, a working thought;
Eagle, high look; wolf secret cruelty:
Monkey, sweet breath; the cow, her fair eyes brought;
The ermine, whitest skin, spotted with nought;
 The sheep, mild-seeming face; climbing, the bear;
 The stag did give the harm-eschewing fear.

The hare, her sleights; the cat, his melancholy;
Ant, industry; and coney,[†] skill to build;
Cranes, order; storks, to be appearing holy;
Chameleon, ease to change; duck, ease to yield;
Crocodile, tears, which might be falsely spill'd:
 Ape great things gave, though he did mowing[†] stand,
 The instrument of instruments, the hand.

Each other beast likewise his present brings:
And (but they drad their prince they oft should want)
They all consented were to give him wings:
And aye more awe towards him for to plant,
To their own work this privilege they grant,
    That from thenceforth to all eternity,
    No beast should freely speak, but only he.

Thus man was made; thus man their lord became:
Who at the first, wanting, or hiding pride,
He did to beasts' best use his cunning frame;
With water drink, herbs meat, and naked hide,
And fellow-like let his dominion slide;
    Not in his saying "I" but "we":
    As if he meant his lordship common[†] be.

But when his seat so rooted he had found,
That they now skill'd not, how from him to wend;
Then gan in guiltless earth full many a wound,[†]
Iron to seek, which 'gainst itself should bend,
To tear the bowels, that good corn should send.
    But yet the common dam none did bemoan;
    Because (though hurt) they never heard her groan.

Then gan he factions in the beasts to breed;
Where helping weaker sort, the nobler beasts,
(As tigers, leopards, bears, and lions' seed)
Disdain'd with this, in deserts sought their rests;
Where famine ravin[†] taught their hungry chests,
    That craftily he forc'd them to do ill,
    Which being done he afterwards would kill,

For murder done, which never erst was seen,
By those great beasts. As for the weaker's good,
He chose themselves his guarders for to been,
'Gainst those of might, of whom in fear they stood,
As horse and dog, not great, but gentle[†] blood:
    Blithe were the common cattle of the field,
    Tho'[†] when they saw their fo'en of greatness kill'd.

But they or spent, or made of slender might,
Then quickly did the meaner cattle find,
The great beams gone, the house on shoulders light:
For by and by the horse fair bits did bind:
The dog was in a collar taught his kind.
    As for the gentle birds, like case might rue,
    When falcon they, and goss-hawk saw in mew.†

Worst fell to smallest birds, and meanest herd,
Whom now his own, full like his own he used.
Yet first but wool, or feathers off he tear'd;
And when they were full us'd to be abused,
For hungry throat their flesh with teeth he bruised:
    At length for glutton taste he did them kill:
    At last for sport their silly lives did spill.

But yet, O man, rage not beyond thy need:
Deem it no glory to swell in tyranny.
Thou art of blood; joy not to make things bleed:
Thou fearest death: think they are loth to die.
A plaint of guiltless hurt doth pierce the sky.
    And you poor beasts, in patience bide your hell,
    Or know your strengths, and then you shall do well.

Thus did I sing, and sing eight sullen hours
To sheep, whom love, not knowledge, made to hear,
Now fancy's fits, now fortune's baleful stours:†
But then I homeward call'd my lambkins dear:
For to my dimmed eyes began to appear
    The night grown old, her black head waxen grey,
    Sure shepherd's sign, that morn should soon fetch day.

Ister the Danube, which flows through Vienna. See Introduction; *couth* knew;
booth hut; *scothe* scarf up (Ringle reads: "sooth"); *welkin* heavens; *ycleped* called;
clerkly rede learned advice; *jump* perfect; *Coriden* possibly a pseudonym for
Sidney's older friend, Edward Wotton. See Introduction and *The Defence of Poesy*;
n'ot know not; *won'd* inhabited; *nis* is not; *once the lion* this passage echoes Isaiah
xi: 6-8; *blaying* bleating; *pewing* crying; *seech* seek; *swink* work; *ounce* leopard;
coney rabbit; *mowing* grimacing; *common* shared; *wound* conventional image of
the fall from the Golden Age; *ravin* preying on each other; *gentle* meek; *tho'*
then; *mew* cage; *stours* storms

3

My true love hath my heart, and I have his,
By just exchange, one for the other giv'n.
I hold his dear, and mine he cannot miss:
There never was a better bargain driv'n.

His heart in me, keeps me and him in one,
My heart in him, his thoughts and senses guides:
He loves my heart, for once it was his own:
I cherish his, because in me it bides.

His heart his wound received from my sight:
My heart was wounded, with his wounded heart,
For as from me, on him his hurt did light,
So still me thought in me his hurt did smart:
    Both equal hurt, in this change sought our bliss:
    My true love hath my heart and I have his.

4*

Lock up, fair lids, the treasures of my heart:
Preserve those beams, this age's only light:
To her sweet sense, sweet sleep, some ease impart,
Her sense too weak to bear her spirit's might.
    And while, O sleep, thou closest up her sight,
(Her sight where love did forge his fairest dart)
O harbour all her parts in easeful plight:
Let no strange dream make her fair body start.
But yet, O dream, if thou wilt not depart
    In this rare subject from thy common right:
    But wilt thyself in such a seat delight,
Then take my shape, and play a lover's part:
    Kiss her from me, and say unto her sprite,
    Till her eyes shine, I live in darkest night.

5

Poor painters oft with silly poets[†] join,
To fill the world with strange but vain conceits:
One brings the stuff, the other stamps the coin,
Which breeds nought else but gloses of deceits.[†]
   Thus painters Cupids paint, thus poets do,
    A naked god, young, blind, with arrows two.

Is he a god, that ever flies the light?
Or naked he, disguis'd in all untruth?
If he be blind, how hitteth he so right?
How is he young, that tam'd old Phoebus'[†] youth?
   But arrows two, and tipt with gold or lead:
    Some, hurt, accuse a third with horny head.[*]

No, nothing so; an old false knave he is,
By Argus got on Io, then a cow:[*]
What time for her Juno her Jove did miss,
And charge of her to Argus did allow.
   Mercury kill'd his false sire for this act,
    His dam a beast was pardon'd beastly fact.[†]

With father's death, and mother's guilty shame,
With Jove's disdain at such a rival's seed,[†]
The wretch compell'd a runagate[†] became,
And learn'd what ill a miser state[†] doth breed,
   To lie, feign, gloze, to steal, pry, and accuse,
    Naught[†] in himself, each other[†] to abuse.

Yet bears he still his parents' stately gifts,
A horned head, cloven foot, and thousand eyes,
Some gazing still, some winking wily shifts,[†]
With long large ears where never rumour dies.
   His horned head doth seem the heaven to spite:
    His cloven foot doth never tread aright.

Thus half a man, with man he eas'ly haunts,
Cloth'd in the shape which soonest may deceive:
Thus half a beast, each beastly vice he plants,
In those weak hearts that his advice receive.
   He prowls each place still in new colours deckt,
   Sucking one's ill, another to infect.

To narrow breasts he comes all wrapt in gain;
To swelling hearts he shines in honour's fire:
To open eyes all beauties he doth rain;
Creeping to each with flattering of desire.
   But for that love's desire most rules the eyes,
   Therein his name,[†] there his chief triumph lies.

Millions of years this old drivel[†] Cupid lives;
While still more wretch, more wicked he doth prove:
Till now at length that Jove him office gives,
(At Juno's suit who much did Argus love)
   In this our world a hangman[†] for to be,
   Of all those fools that will have all they see.

poor incompetent; *silly* ignorant; *gloses of deceits* deceitful appearances; *old Phoebus*
Cupid caused Phoebus to fall in love with Daphne; *fact* deed, crime; *seed* offspring;
runagate vagabond; *ill* wickedness; *miser state* wretchedness; *naught* wicked;
each other everyone else; *winking wily shifts* turning a blind eye to lovers' wily
tricks; *name* "Cupiditas" – desire (of the eyes) or reputation; *drivel* old rascal;
hang-man lowest, most debased profession

6*

Let mother earth now deck herself in flowers,
To see her offspring seek a good increase,
Where justest love doth vanquish Cupid's powers
And war of thoughts is swallow'd up in peace
   Which never may decrease
   But like the turtles fair[†]
Live one in two, a well united pair,
   Which that no chance may stain,
O Hymen long their coupled joys maintain.

O heav'n, awake, show forth thy stately face,
Let not these slumb'ring clouds thy beauties hide,
But with thy cheerful presence help to grace
The honest bridegroom, and the bashful bride,
   Whose loves may ever bide,
   Like to the elm and vine,
With mutual embracements them to twine:
   In which delightful pain,
O Hymen, long their coupled joys maintain.

Ye Muses all, which chaste affects[†] allow,
And have to Lalus show'd your secret skill,
To this chaste love your sacred favours bow,
And so to him and her your gifts distil
   That they all vice may kill:
   And like to lilies pure
Do please all eyes, and spotless do endure,
   Where that all bliss may reign:
O Hymen, long their coupled joys maintain.

Ye Nymphs, which in the waters empire have,
Since Lalus' music oft doth yield you praise,
Grant to the thing which we for Lalus crave.
Let one time (but long first) close up their days,
   One grave their bodies seize:
   And like two rivers sweet,
When they though divers do together meet:
   One stream both streams contain,
O Hymen, long their coupled joys maintain.

Pan, father Pan, the god of silly sheep,
Whose care is cause that they in number grow,
Have much more care of them that them do keep,
Since from these good the others' good doth flow,
   And make their issue show
   In number like the herd
Of younglings, which thyself with love hast rear'd,
   Or like the drops of rain.
O Hymen, long their coupled joys maintain.

161

Virtue, (if not a god) yet God's chief part,
Be thou the knot of this their open vow,
That still he be her head, she be his heart,
He lean to her, she unto him do bow:
    Each other still allow:[†]
    Like oak and mistletoe,
Her strength from him, his praise from her do grow.
    In which most lovely train,[†]
O Hymen, long their coupled joys maintain.

But thou foul Cupid, sire to lawless lust,
Be thou far hence with thy empoison'd dart,
Which though of glitt'ring gold, shall here take rust
Where simple love, which chasteness doth impart,
    Avoids thy hurtful art,
    Not needing charming skill,
Such minds with sweet affections for to fill:
    Which being pure and plain,
O Hymen, long their coupled joys maintain.

All churlish words, shrewd answers, crabbed looks,
All privateness, self-seeking, inward spite,
All waywardness, which nothing kindly brooks,
All strife for toys, and claiming master's right:
    Be hence aye put to flight.
    All stirring husband's hate
'Gainst neighbours good, for womanish debate,[†]
    Be fled as thing most vain;
O Hymen, long their coupled joys maintain.

All peacock pride, and fruits of peacock pride,
Longing to be with loss of substance gay
With recklessness[†] what may thy house betide,
So that you may on higher slippers stay,
    Forever hence away!
    Yet let not sluttery,
The sink of filth, be counted huswifery,
    But keeping wholesome mean:[†]
O Hymen, long their coupled joys maintain.

But above all, away vile jealousy,
The evil of evils, just cause to be unjust.
(How can he love, suspecting treachery?
How can she love where love cannot win trust?)
   Go, snake, hide thee in dust,
   Ne dare once show thy face,
Where open hearts do hold so constant place,
   That they thy sting restrain:
O Hymen, long their coupled joys maintain.

The earth is deckt with flowers, the heav'ns display'd,
Muses grant gifts, nymphs long and joined life,
Ran store of babes, virtue their thoughts well staid;
Cupid's lust gone, and gone is bitter strife,
   Happy man, happy wife.
   No pride shall them oppress,
Nor yet shall yield to loathsome sluttishness,
   And jealousy is slain:
For Hymen will their coupled joys maintain.

turtles turtle doves (symbols of constancy); *affects* affections, emotions; *each . . . allow* let each always bear with the other; *train* course; *nothing . . . brooks* takes nothing kindly; *stirring . . . womanish debate* women's quarrels provoking friction between a husband and his good neighbours; *recklessness* neglect; *wholesome mean* healthy middle way

7*

STREPHON   KLAIUS

Strephon: Ye goat-herd gods, that love the grassy mountains,
             Ye nymphs which haunt the springs in pleasant valleys,
             Ye satyrs joy'd with free and quiet forests,
             Vouchsafe your silent ears to plaining[†] music,
             Which to my woes gives still an early morning:
             And draws the dolour on till weary evening.

Klaius: O Mercury, foregoer to the evening,
             O heavenly huntress of the savage mountains,[†]
             O lovely star, entitl'd of the morning,[†]
             While that my voice doth fill these woeful valleys,

163

Vouchsafe your silent ears to plaining music,
Which oft hath Echo tir'd in secret forests.

Strephon: I that was once free-burgess of the forests,
Where shade from sun, and sport I sought in evening,
I that was once esteem'd for pleasant music,
Am banisht now among the monstrous mountains
Of huge despair, and foul affliction's valleys,
Am grown a screech-owl to myself each morning.

Klaius: I that was once delighted every morning,
Hunting the wild inhabiters of forests,
I that was once the music of these valleys,
So darkened am, that all my day is evening;
Heart-broken so, that mole-hills seem high mountains,
And fill the vales with cries instead of music.

Strephon: Long since, alas, my deadly swannish music[†]
Hath made itself a crier of the morning,
And hath with wailing strength climb'd highest
    mountains;
Long since my thoughts more desert be than forests;
Long since I see my joys come to their evening,
And state thrown down to over-trodden valleys.

Klaius: Long since the happy dwellers of these valleys
Have pray'd me leave my strange exclaiming music,
Which troubles their day's work, and joys of evening;
Long since I hate the night, more hate the morning:
Long since my thoughts chase me like beasts in forests,
And make me wish myself laid under mountains.

Strephon: Meseems I see the high and stately mountains,
Transform themselves to low dejected valleys;
Meseems I hear in these ill-changed forests
The nightingales do learn of owls their music;
Meseems I feel the comfort of the morning
Turn'd to the mortal serene[†] of an evening.

Klaius:	Meseems I see a filthy cloudy evening As soon as sun begins to climb the mountains; Meseems I feel a noisome scent, the morning, When I do smell the flowers of these valleys; Meseems I hear, when I do hear sweet music, The dreadful cries of murder'd men in forests.
Strephon:	I wish to fire the trees of all these forests; I give the sun a last farewell each evening; I curse the fidding finders out of music; With envy I do hate the lofty mountains, And with despite despise the humble valleys; I do detest night, evening, day, and morning.
Klaius:	Curse to myself my prayer is, the morning: My fire is more, than can be made with forests; My state more base, than are the basest valleys; I wish no evenings more to see, each evening; Shamed, I hate myself in sight of mountains, And stop mine ears, lest I grow mad with music.
Strephon:	For she, whose parts maintain'd a perfect music, Whose beauty shin'd more than the blushing morning, Who much did pass in state the stately mountains, In straightness pass'd the cedars of the forests, Hath cast me, wretch, into eternal evening, By taking her two suns from these dark valleys.
Klaius:	For she, with whom compar'd, the Alps are valleys, She, whose least word brings from the spheres their music, At whose approach the sun rose in the evening, Who, where she went, bare in her forehead morning, Is gone, is gone from these our spoiled forests, Turning to deserts our best pastur'd mountains.
Strephon:	These mountains witness shall, so shall these valleys,

Klaius:　　　These forests eke,[†] made wretched by our music,
　　　　　Our morning hymn this is, and song at evening.

8*

　　　Why dost thou haste away
　　　O Titan fair, the giver of the day?
　　　Is it to carry news
　　　To western wights, what stars in east appear?
　　　Or dost thou think that here
　　　Is left a sun,[†] whose beams thy place may use?
　　　Yet stay and well peruse,
　　　What be her gifts, that make her equal thee,
　　　Bend all thy light to see
　　　In earthly clothes enclos'd a heavenly spark.
　　　Thy running course cannot such beauties mark:
　　　No, no, thy motions be
　　　Hastened from us with bar of shadow dark,
　　　Because that thou, the author of our sight,
　　　Disdain'st we see thee stain'd[†] with other's light.

9*

The nightingale, as soon as April bringeth
Unto her rested sense a perfect waking,
While late bare earth, proud of new clothing springeth,
Sings out her woes, a thorn her song-book making:
　　And mournfully bewailing,
　　Her throat in tunes expresseth
　　What grief her breast oppresseth,
For Tereus' force on her chaste will prevailing.
O Philomela fair, O take some gladness,
That here is juster cause of plaintful sadness:
　　Thine earth now springs, mine fadeth;
Thy thorn without, my thorn my heart invadeth.

Alas, she hath no other cause of anguish
But Tereus' love, on her by strong hand wroken,[†]
Wherein she suff'ring all her spirits' languish
Full womanlike complains her will was broken.
   But I who daily craving,
   Cannot have to content me,[†]
   Have more cause to lament me,
Since wanting is more woe than too much having.
O Philomela fair, O take some gladness,
That here is juster cause of plaintful sadness:
   Thine earth now springs, mine fadeth;
Thy thorn without, my thorn my heart invadeth.

wroken inflicted; *cannot ... me* cannot have what would please me

10*

Thou blind man's mark,[†] thou fool's self chosen snare,
Fond fancy's scum, and dregs of scatter'd thought,
Band[†] of all evils, cradle of causeless care,
Thou web of will, whose end is never wrought;

Desire, desire I have too dearly bought,
With price of mangled mind thy worthless ware,
Too long, too long asleep thou hast me brought,
Who should my mind to higher things prepare.

But yet in vain thou hast my ruin sought,
In vain thou madest me to vain things aspire,
In vain thou kindlest all thy smoky fire;

For virtue hath this bitter lesson taught,
Within myself to seek my only hire:[†]
Desiring nought but how to kill desire.

mark target; *band* swaddling band; *hire* reward

11

Leave me, O Love, which reachest but to dust,
And thou my mind aspire to higher things:
Grow rich in that which never taketh rust:
What ever fades, but fading pleasure brings.

Draw in thy beams, and humble all thy might,
To that sweet yoke, where lasting freedoms be:
Which breaks the clouds and opens forth the light,
That doth both shine and give us sight to see.

O take fast hold, let that light be thy guide,
In this small course which birth draws out to death,
And think how evil becometh him to slide,
Who seeketh heav'n, and comes of heav'nly breath.
  Then farewell world, thy uttermost I see,
  Eternal Love maintain thy life in me.

Splendidis longum valedico nugis.

Notes

Astrophil and Stella

Sonnet 9: *touch* touchstone   1. a fine-grained black quartz used to test the quality of gold and silver alloy; 2. associated with jet which, when charged by friction, attracts light materials like straw.

Sonnet 30: crammed with topical allusions. *New-moon* alludes to the crescent on the Turkish flag; the Turks were thought to be preparing to attack Spain; *king* Maximilian II had claimed the Polish throne and invaded Muscovy; *three parts* French politics were seen as divided between Catholics, Protestants and *politiques*; *Orange tree* William the Silent (see Introduction) had ruled Holland since 1576, but in 1581-2 had lost some towns to the Spanish; *golden bit* alludes to a levy imposed on Irish landowners by Sir Henry Sidney.

Sonnet 31: *ungratefulness* a difficult construction: 1. do those above call (the lady's) ungratefulness a virtue? or 2. since "ungrateful" means "unpleasant" is it that the lover's Virtue is considered unpleasing there?

Sonnet 45: *new doubts* seems to mean: his honourable behaviour, which results in "servant's wrack", only creates in her new doubts or fears.

Sonnet 75: A complexly "knowing" poem, based on analogies with the times and person of King Edward IV, who seized the throne from Henry VI. The chronicles depict him as violent and bad-tempered, so Sidney's tongue may be firmly in his cheek. *Flouredelouce* fleur-de-lys, royal emblem of France, threatened by Edward's troops, so that Louis XI ("witty Lewis") paid tribute; *bloody lion* red lion of Scotland, with whom Edward negotiated a truce; *lose . . . love* Edward briefly lost his throne to "Kingmaker" Warwick, when he ignored Warwick's efforts to arrange a marriage for him and married Lady Elizabeth Gray, his own choice.

Sonnet 80: *grain* 1. Originally, a scarlet colour. 2. to dye something in the grain is to dye it fast or thoroughly.

Third song: *boy . . . Grecian maid* both stories from Pliny: the boy, Thoas was rescued from robbers by a dragon he had raised; the maid tamed an eagle which brought her food and eventually chose to die on her funeral pyre.

The Defence of Poesy

Emperor's Court see Introduction, p.12

Musaeus legendary, pre-Homeric poet; *Homer* more or less legendary author of the *Iliad* and *Odyssey*, supposed author of the much later Homeric Hymns; *Hesiod* fl. 8th Century B.C., author of *Theogony* and *Works and Days*; *Orpheus* archetypal poet/ singer, probably pre-Homeric and not the author of the later Orphic writings attributed to him; *Linus* supposed master of Orpheus, son of a Muse; *Amphion* son of Zeus and Antiope, a legendary musician, whose lyre was said to have moved the stones of Thebes at its foundation; *Livius Andronicus* (c.284-04 B.C.), earliest Latin poet, Greek by birth; *Ennius* see below

Thales (fl. 585 B.C.) author of lost works on nautical astronomy and first causes; *Empedocles* (fl. 450 B.C.), fragments of his poems, "On Nature" and "Purifications" survive; *Parmenides* (fl. 475 B.C.) founder of the Eleatic school of philosophy; *Pythagoras* (fl. 530 B.C.) actually left nothing in writing, for reasons of secrecy – Sidney is probably thinking of the so-called Golden Sayings wrongly attributed to him; *Phocylidis* (fl.560 B.C.) a gnomic poet; *Tyrtaeus* (fl. 670 B.C.) an Athenian, possibly a lame schoolmaster, whose poetry inspired the Spartans to victory; *Solon* (fl. 600 B.C.) Athenian legislator

Gyges' Ring see Plato, *Republic* II, Cicero, *De Officiis* III

History the *History* of the "father of history" was divided into nine books, each named after a Muse, by later Alexandrian scholars.

Sortes Virgilianae opening the works of Virgil at random and "applying" the first verses the eye falls upon, as some people do with the Bible

Albinus acclaimed Emperor of Rome by his troops in A.D. 193, defeated and killed in 197

Arma . . . armis frantic, I seize arms, but there is little point in arms

brazen invokes the literary tradition of the Four Ages of Man – the golden (perfect) age, the silver, bronze (ruled over by Jove) and iron, in which we live now

Theagenes see below, under Heliodorus; *Pylades* friend of Orestes in the Greek tragedies; *Orlando* Roland in the European chivalric romances, Orlando in Ariosto's *Orlando Furioso*; *Xenophon's Cyrus* the exemplary hero of Xenophon's political treatise, the *Cyropaedia*; *Aeneas* survivor of Troy and founder of Rome in Virgil's *Aeneid*

Emanuel Tremillius and Franciscus Junius producers in the 1570s of a Protestant Latin Bible

Tyrtaeus, Phocylidis see above; *Cato* Dionysius Cato, author of the *Distychs*; *Lucretius* Latin author of *De Rerum Natura*; *Virgil's "Georgics"* seen as a treatise on agriculture; *Manilius* author of an astrological treatise, *Astronomica*; *Pontanus* Giovanni Pontano (1426-1503), soldier, statesman, scholar, Latin poet of *Urania*, on the stars; *Lucan* Roman author of *Pharsalia*, on the wars between Caesar and Pompey

Lucretia raped by Tarquin, type of the honourable suicide

contains singular for plural, common in Elizabethan English

testis . . . vetustatis the witness of the ages, the light of truth, the life of memory, the governess of life, the herald of antiquity (Cicero, *De Oratore* II)

Brutus killer of Julius Caesar; *Alphonsus of Aragon* extravagant but enlightened ruler *formidine... amore* by the terror of punishment than by the love of virtue

Tully Marcus Tullius Cicero, Roman orator and politician; *Anchises* father of Aeneas (see above); *Ulysses/Calypso* in the *Odyssey;* *Sophocles* in fact these events are reported, not shown on stage, in *Ajax; Ulysses, Diomedes, Achilles, Nisus, Euryalus* characters in the stories of the Trojan wars; *Oedipus* in the plays by Sophocles or Seneca; *Agamemnon* in the plays by Aeschylus or Seneca (*Atreus* was his father); *Theban brothers* twin sons of Oedipus; *Medea* witch who took revenge on Jason when he deserted her; *Gnatho* parasite; *Pandarus* the go-between, "pander", in *Troilus and Criseyde*

Mediocribus... columnae neither gods, nor men, nor even booksellers have ever put up with poets of middling ability (Horace, *The Art of Poetry*)

Cyrus in Xenophon see above; *Justin* author of *Histories* some time in the Christian era, factually worthless but without Xenophon's avowed exemplary intent; *Dares Phrygius* mentioned in the *Iliad,* traditionally supposed to have written a Trojan version of the fall of Troy; *Canidia* ugly witch, mentioned several times by Horace

Tantalus punished in hell by never being able to eat the fruit or drink the water that was so close to him (hence "tantalise"); *Alexander, Quintus Curtius* Quintus Curtius (1st Century A.D.) wrote a sensational life of Alexander the Great; *Scipio* Africanus, general who defeated Hannibal, later accused of political malpractice

Miltiades victor of Marathon, subsequently imprisoned by his own people; *Phocion* Athenian general and patriot, condemned to drink poison for impiety and corrupting youth; *cruel Severus* Lucius Septimius Severus, emperor 193-211, ruthlessly disposed of several rivals; *excellent Severus* Alexander Severus, emperor 222-35, killed in a mutiny; *Sylla* (138-78 B.C.), dictator of Rome; *Marius* (157-86 B.C.), great rival of the former, their conflicts divided Italy for twenty years; *Cato* Cato of Utica, an unbending, aristocratic Stoic and critic of Caesar

Fugientem...est in the last book of the *Aeneid*, Turnus, king of the Rutuli, anticipates the disasters to come: "shall this land see Turnus flying hence? Is death indeed so miserable?"

Sannazzarro Jacopo Sannazzarro (1455-1530), author of a mixed prose-and-verse *Arcadia*, one of Sidney's own models; *Boethius* c.480-524, author of the highly influential *Consolation of Philosophy*

Meliboeus in the first Eclogue of Virgil, Meliboeus laments the seizure of his land and animals, while Tityrus rejoices that he is protected by the emperor

Haec...nobis Virgil Eclogue VII tells of a singing contest between Thyrsis and Corydon: "I remember this and how Thyrsis, vanquished, strove in vain; from that day, it is Corydon, Corydon for us"

Omne...amico; circum...ludit a more or less continuous quotation from Persius, on Horatian satire: "(Horace) craftily probes every fault of his friend, while making him laugh, and once inside plays around the secrets of his heart"

Est...aequus Even in Ulubrae (happiness is to be found) if an equable mind does not fail us (Horace, *Epistles* I.xi)

Qui...redit The cruel ruler who governs his dominions harshly fears those who fear him; terror rebounds on its author (Seneca, *Oedipus*)

Tydeus in Statius, *Thebais*; *Rinaldo* in Ariosto's *Orlando Furioso* and Tasso's *Gerusalemme Liberata*

melius...Crantore praising (Homer) as a better teacher than Chrysippus (an early Stoic philosopher) and Crantor (an early commentator on Plato)

Agrippa Cornelius Agrippa in *Vanity of the Arts*; *Erasmus* in *In Praise of Folly*. The irony of both works might be missed by the unwary

173

Percontatorem... est Flee the inquisitive man; for that man cannot hold his tongue (Horace, *Epistles* I. xviii); *Dum...sumus* while each man pleases himself, we are a credulous crowd (Ovid, *Remedium Amoris*)

quiddity essential nature; *ens* pure being; *prima materia* first matter – all terms from scholastic philosophy

Ennius the earliest of the Roman poets, who accompanied the consul M. Fulvius Nobilior to battle in Greece; this displeased Cato the Censor (as distinct from his great grandson, Cato of Utica)

Dionysius Dionysius the Elder (c.432-367 B.C.), tyrant of Syracuse, said to have had a hand in delivering Plato into slavery

twice two St Paul is said to draw on four Greek poets, Aratus, Cleanthes, Epimenides and Menander

Qua... exigendos certain rough and barbarous men wish to abuse his authority to banish poets from the republic

Musa...laeso Muse, relate to me through what offended power... (*Aeneid*, I)

Adrian the Roman emperor, Hadrian (117-138 A.D.) a writer of verse; *Germanicus* Germanicus Caesar, popular general and adopted son of Emperor Tiberius; *Robert* Robert II of Anjou, patron of Petrarch; *Francis* Francis I (1494-1547), patron of French art and literature; *James* either James I or James VI of Scotland (the latter became James I of England)
Hospital Michel de l'Hopital, Chancellor of France 1560-68
Epaminondas Theban general who transformed the menial office of sanitation official to one of great respect

Queis... Titan whose hearts Titan had shaped of better clay (adapted from Juvenal, *Satires* XIV)

Daedalus mythical first artist; he and his son, Icarus, flew with wings attached by wax, but the latter flew too close to the sun, the wax melted, and he was drowned in the Aegean

Quicquid...erit whatever I try to say will turn out as verse

Mirror of Magistrates miscellany of stories on the "fall of princes" theme, first published 1559; *Surrey* executed by Henry VIII; his Petrarchan lyrics and translations of parts of the *Aeneid* were models for the Elizabethans; *Shepherd's Calendar* pastoral poems, dedicated to Sidney – first major work published (1579) by Edmund Spenser; *Theocritus...Sannazzarro* regarded as the best models for pastoral poetry

Gorboduc by Sackville and Norton, first performed 1561 before Queen Elizabeth, on themes of civil war and dynastic rivalry, based on early British legends; *Seneca* Roman tragedian, whose ten tragedies were the supreme models for the Renaissance

Pacolet's horse a flying horse, which appears in the romance, *Valentine and Orson* (1489)

Nil...facit Poverty has no harsher misfortune within it than that it makes men ridiculous (Juvenal, *Satires* III)

Nizolian Nizolius was author of a handbook of Ciceronian phrases, slavishly followed by some stylists

Vivit...venit He lives. Lives? Verily, he even comes into this Senate.... (Cicero, *Against Catiline* I)

both probably Latin and Greek, the two "venerable" sources of English, though French and German were more immediate

Si possunt if my songs can do it (*Aeneid* IX)

Midas given asses' ears for preferring the music of Pan to that of Apollo; *Bubonax* an odd slip by Sidney, apparently conflating two names, Hipponax, a satiric poet, and Bupalus, a sculptor

Miscellaneous Poems

MP 1. One of several early poems to "Mira", not originally in the

Arcadia, but inserted among the Third Eclogues by the editor of the 1593 edition as an example of the "country songs" of Philisides – Sidney's name for himself in his romance – who, it is explained, "to show what a stranger he was to himself, spake of himself as of a third person". The song it contains is the earliest English example of a *canzone*, imitated from the Italian of Sannazzarro (see *The Defence of Poesy*, p.139). The short penultimate stanza, "My song...", is the "envoy", in which Philisides consigns the song to Mira, who is supposed to be beyond the hills, to the West. The final stanza is set apart from the others in using feminine rhymes throughout. The poem was perhaps paired with the next one to show the range of Sidney/Philisides's achievement in pastoral poetry.

MP 2. Philisides – Sidney himself – sings this song during wedding festivities, rather than dwell on his own misfortunes in love (see the previous poem and note). It is a political allegory in the form of a beast fable, and deals with some sensitive issues: the creation of monarchy (man), its descent into tyranny, the alienation of the aristocracy (the nobler beasts), and the ruthless exploitation of the commons (the weaker beasts who initially applaud what happens to the stronger ones). It is clearly a call for a stronger aristocracy as the best defence against tyranny. Sidney credits Languet (see Introduction) with teaching him the song, and perhaps sets it on the banks of the Ister (the Danube) to point up the application of the piece to the growth of despotism in Continental states like Spain and France – at any rate, away from England. It is perhaps a measure of the political delicacy of the piece that the 1590 edition of the *Arcadia* ascribed it to a nameless "young shepherd" and placed it among the First Eclogues at the end of Book 1. But it clearly belongs among the Third Eclogues at the end of Book 3, where other marriage poems discuss the nature of the best government for families. The poem uses many archaisms – "words fit to frame a pastoral style" as some of the listeners in the *Arcadia* note; this is unusual in Sidney, and he repudiated the convention in *The Defence of Poesy* (see p.139).

MP 3. A song of the paradoxical pleasures and pains of love, in sonnet form, which has achieved fame outside the *Arcadia*. There (Book 3, Chapter 37) it has a comic context, supposedly sung by a young and beautiful shepherdess (Charita) to the old and ugly Dametas; but we only have the word of Musidorus for this, and he is anxious to get Dametas's wife, Miso, out of the way so that he can pursue his own elopement with Pamela. His invented tale and its pretty song succeed, since Miso rushes off to prevent a further supposed assignation between "Charita" and Dametas.

MP 4. From the *Arcadia*, Book 3, Chapter 38. Musidorus sings Pamela to sleep with this sonnet/song, which has only two rhyme sounds.

MP 5. In the *Old Arcadia* a satire on love by the grave shepherd, Dicus, explicating, in emblem-fashion, his picture of Cupid, and placed among the First Eclogues. Transferred, in the revised *Arcadia*, to Miso, the old-hag wife of Dametas (Book 2, Chapter 14), in which context its heterodoxy is the more easily discounted.
gold, lead, horny the golden arrow kindles love, the leaden disdain; the horny arrow of cuckoldry is Sidney's invention.
Argus Jove seduced Io, who was transformed into a heifer (to deceive Juno) and guarded by hundred-eyed Argus, who was slain by Mercury. See Ovid, *Metamorphoses* i, 588ff. It is Sidney's joke that Argus begot Cupid.

MP 6. Sung by Dicus in the Third Eclogue of the *Old Arcadia*, to celebrate the marriage of Lalus and Kala, a shepherd and shepherdess. It is the earliest formal epithalamium, or marriage-song, in English; there are famous later examples by Spenser and Donne. The stanza is based on a Spanish song by Gil Polo.

MP 7. Originally in the Fourth Eclogues of the *Old Arcadia*, but shuffled about in later versions. The shepherds, Strephon and Klaius, mourn the departure of Urania, whom they both love, from Arcadia. The poem is a double sestina (a sestina is a six-stanza poem, in which each stanza has only six lines and uses the same six words to end its line, albeit in a rolling sequence),

177

with a final three-line envoy which recapitulates the six end-words. The poem is, however, far more than a demonstration of technical virtuosity and has been widely admired by, for example, William Empson (in *Seven Types of Ambiguity*) and John Crowe Ransom (in *The New Criticism*).

MP 8. One of the earliest madrigals in English, contained in Book 3 of the *Old Arcadia*, where it is sung by Basilius about Cleophila (in later versions, Zelmane) – actually Pyrocles in disguise.

MP 9. From *Certain Sonnets*, a collection of poems probably put together by Sidney himself, possibly as early as 1580, and circulated in manuscript. First published in the 1598 folio of Sidney's works. Philomela was ravished by Tereus, who cut out her tongue to preserve his secret; she was transformed into a nightingale, which a later tradition claimed sings with its breast against a thorn. Sidney, not without some humour, compares his lot with hers.

MP 10, 11. These sonnets are the last two pieces in *Certain Sonnets* (see note above) and demonstrate most clearly the serious piety that lies beneath Sidney's writing.
Splendidis...nugis I bid a long farewell to splendid trifles.

"The Fyfield Books series provides an admirable service in publishing good inexpensive selections from the works of interesting but neglected poets"
— *British Book News*

THOMAS LOVELL BEDDOES (1803-49)
Selected Poems
edited by Judith Higgens

THE BRONTË SISTERS
Selected Poems
edited by Stevie Davies

ELIZABETH BARRETT BROWNING (1806-61)
Selected Poems
edited by Malcolm Hicks

THOMAS CAMPION (1567-1620)
Ayres and Observations
edited by Joan Hart

GEORGE CHAPMAN (?1559-1634)
Selected Poems
edited by Eirean Wain

THOMAS CHATTERTON (1752-70)
Selected Poems
edited by Grevel Lindop

CHARLES COTTON (1630-87)
Selected Poems
edited by Ken Robinson

WILLIAM COWPER (1731-1800)
Selected Poems
edited by Nick Rhodes

GEORGE CRABBE (1754-1832)
Selected Poems
edited by Jem Poster

RICHARD CRASHAW (1612/13-49)
Selected Poems
edited by Michael Cayley

MICHAEL DRAYTON (1563-1631)
Selected Poems
edited by Vivian Thomas

GEORGE GASCOIGNE (1530-77)
The Green Knight:
selected poems and prose
edited by Roger Pooley

JOHN GAY (1685-1732)
Selected Poems
edited by Marcus Walsh

JOHN GOWER (1330-1408)
Selected Poetry
edited by Carole Weinberg

THOMAS GRAY (1716-71)
Selected Poems
edited by John Heath-Stubbs

ROBERT HENRYSON (1425?-1508?)
Selected Poems
edited by W.R.J. Barron

ROBERT HERRICK (1591-1674)
Selected Poems
edited by David Jesson-Dibley

THOMAS HOCCLEVE (?1348-1430)
Selected Poems
edited by Bernard O'Donoghue

BEN JONSON (1572-1637)
Epigrams & The Forest
edited by Richard Dutton

WALTER SAVAGE LANDOR (1775-1864)
Selected Poems and Prose
edited by Keith Hanley

ANDREW MARVELL (1621-78)
Selected Poems
edited by Bill Hutchings

GEORGE MEREDITH (1828-1909)
Selected Poems
edited by Keith Hanley

CHARLES OF ORLEANS (1394-1465)
Selected Poems
edited by Sally Purcell

SIR WALTER RALEGH (?1554-1618)
Selected Writings
edited by Gerald Hammond

JOHN WILMOT, EARL OF ROCHESTER
(1648-80)
The Debt to Pleasure
edited by John Adlard

CHRISTINA ROSSETTI (1830-94)
Selected Poems
edited by C.H. Sisson

SIR PHILIP SIDNEY (1554-86)
Selected Poetry and Prose
edited by Richard Dutton

JOHN SKELTON (1460-1529)
Selected Poems
edited by Gerald Hammond

CHRISTOPHER SMART (1722-71)
Selected Poems
edited by Marcus Walsh

DONALD STANFORD (editor)
Three Poets of the Rhymers' Club:
Lionel Johnson, Ernest Dowson,
John Davidson

HENRY HOWARD, EARL OF SURREY
(1517-47)
Selected Poems
edited by Dennis Keene

JONATHAN SWIFT (1667-1745)
Selected Poems
edited by C.H. Sisson

ALGERNON CHARLES SWINBURNE
(1837-1909)
Selected Poems
edited by L.M. Findlay

ARTHUR SYMONS (1865-1945)
Selected Writings
edited by R.V. Holdsworth

THOMAS TRAHERNE (?1637-74)
Selected Writings
edited by Dick Davis

HENRY VAUGHAN (1622-95)
Selected Poems
edited by Robert B. Shaw

ANNE FINCH, COUNTESS OF WINCHILSEA
(1661-1720)
Selected Poems
edited by Denys Thompson

EDWARD YOUNG (1683-1765)
Selected Poems
edited by Brian Hepworth

"Carcanet are doing an excellent job in this series: the editions are labours of love, not just commercial enterprises. I hope they are familiar to all readers and teachers of literature." – *Times Literary Supplement*